CW00968758

Bringing Out the Best in Your **Wife**

H. NORMAN WRIGHT

Includes Small-Group Study Questions

Bringing Out the Best in Your **Wife**

Regal

From Gospel Light
Ventura, California, U.S.A.

Published by Regal
From Gospel Light
Ventura, California, U.S.A.
www.regalbooks.com
Printed in the U.S.A.

Library of Congress Cataloging-in-Publication Data
Wright, H. Norman.
Bringing out the best in your wife : encourage your spouse and experience the
relationship you've always wanted / H. Norman Wright.
p. cm.
ISBN 978-0-8307-5216-4 (hardcover)
1. Husbands—Religious life. 2. Wives—Psychology. 3. Encouragement—Religious
aspects—Christianity. 4. Marriage—Religious aspects—Christianity. I. Title.
BV4528.3.W55 2010
248.8'44—dc22
2009049112

1 2 3 4 5 6 7 8 9 10 / 15 14 13 12 11 10

Rights for publishing this book outside the U.S.A. or in non-English languages are
administered by Gospel Light Worldwide, an international not-for-profit ministry.
For additional information, please visit www.glww.org, email info@glww.org, or write
to Gospel Light Worldwide, 1957 Eastman Avenue, Ventura, CA 93003, U.S.A.

Contents

1. Believe in Your Wife 7

2. Husbands Speak Out 33

3. Wives Speak Out 59

4. Understand Your Wife 91

5. Romancing Your Wife 111

6. God's Plan for Husbands 135

7. Questions Men Ask 153

8. The Power of a Praying Man 183

9. Some Concluding Thoughts 209

Endnotes 215

1

Believe in **Your Wife**

FROM TIME TO TIME, I'VE ASKED HUSBANDS THE QUESTION, "If your wife were to change something about herself, what would you like to see changed?" You can just imagine all the different answers I've received over the years; they've ranged from the most absurd and ridiculous to those that are quite positive and encouraging. Now and then I've heard, "Nope. It can't be done. She'd never change." Once in a while I've heard, "I'd like my wife to value herself more. I'd like her to see herself as God sees her. She has so much potential under the surface. I'd like to see that develop." Now there's a great answer! This husband wants his wife to become the best she can be. Is it possible? Yes! Can she do it on her own? No! Can you, as a husband, change your wife? Yes *and* no! You can't do it *for* her or force it to happen. But you can encourage change to happen. You have more influence on and power over change than you can imagine.

The bottom line is this: What you believe about your wife will determine what she becomes. When Ephesians 5:25 states that a husband is to love his wife as Christ loved the church (to love her sacrificially), it also means he's her cheerleader.

Every husband is given a power that can bring about change, growth and the fulfillment of potential in his wife. There's so much truth to these words:

No matter how beautiful a woman is, she will struggle with not liking something about herself. No matter how confident a woman seems, insecurities still haunt her at times. No matter how fulfilled a woman is in her calling in life, there will always be a part of her that wonders if she measures up. Some women struggle more than others, but all women long to be affirmed, appreciated and admired. Other than God, there's no one who can do more to build a woman's self-esteem than her husband. Your wife is in the process of becoming what you think of her![1]

When a wife tells her husband, "Thank you for believing in me," her husband is fulfilling his calling.

Have you heard those words from your wife? Does she ever turn to you and say, "Thank you for bringing out the best in me"? Does she say, "It's your encouragement that makes my life different"? Read what these wives say about how their husbands bring out the best in them:

He appreciates me! He tells me often how much I mean to him, and he thanks me for things I do for him. He compliments me in front of other people, especially in front of our children; when he does that I feel valued and loved. He believes in me! He validates my dreams—and believes I can do whatever God has called me to do. He never trivializes my role as a woman—but treats me as a true equal.

He believes in me. Shows compassion. Uses humor to defuse a disagreement. Is not afraid to admit he is wrong. Compliments me often. Likes my cooking. Talks to me. Listens to me. Makes me feel important. He would even watch a chick flick with me. He keeps himself healthy and looking good. Takes dancing lessons with me and then takes me dancing. Brings me flowers. Leaves me notes in my snack bag.

My husband is a wonderful listener. He has learned over the years that the way I process problems is by "fleshing them out" out loud—or talking them through. It helps just to have his undivided attention, and then the solution will come to me. I don't necessarily need the problem solved; just an ear.

He truly knows me and wants me to be the best God made me to be. We are so opposite from each other in most things, but we accept each other and don't try to change one another. He studies me—my needs, my desires, my strengths, weaknesses, joys, sorrows; and he meets those needs whenever and however he is led to. He encourages by words and actions, exhorts where necessary and treats me like I am God's gift to him. I am free to flourish as the person God made me to be without fear of taking anything away from my husband. I am so grateful!

Not all the responses from wives are positive. Some wives lament the lack of encouragement in their lives. Read some responses from wives who describe what they wish their husbands wouldn't do:

[I wish he wouldn't] get angry so easily over things that don't go his way, or when we disagree about something.

He tends to overreact and blow up over the smallest things. It makes him an unsafe person, and I can't relax and just be myself. I wonder when "Mount Vesuvius" will erupt next. It shuts down communication and damages intimacy and closeness.

Sometimes he gets into his sarcastic "guy talk" mode where everything is a "dig" or a negative comment (because with his years in the military, that is how they communicate). I wish he wouldn't talk that way to me. It's hard for him when coming out of that environment to adjust to home.

I really hate it when he dictates to me, like I'm an employee. It makes me feel like I'm stupid. I'm a highly educated woman, yet he can make me feel so stupid. I really hate it when he treats our kids badly. This is an issue with us. He seems to favor one over the other, and it really creates tension for us.

He makes promises and does not follow through. He often gets sidetracked and forgets what he promised me. This hurts my heart. Also he is so prideful when he knows he has hurt my feelings; he would rather wait out my hurt and resentment than come to me and ask forgiveness or talk things out, for he knows I will "get over it." But what he really does not know is that until it's resolved, the hurt and resentment are still there.

I wish he wouldn't walk away to do his thing when I'm in the middle of a conversation with him—for example,

he checks emails, phone messages or DVR programs—
and then comes back to me and expects to continue
where I left off when he decided to leave the room.

Many husbands do try to encourage their wives, and even
think they are doing so. But it's difficult to be an encourager if
you don't understand what encouragement really means.

ENCOURAGEMENT DEFINED

To be an encourager you need to have an attitude of optimism.
The *American Heritage Dictionary* has one of the better definitions of the word "optimist." It's a "tendency or disposition to
expect the best possible outcome, or to dwell on the most hope-
ful aspect of a situation." When this is your attitude or perspective, you'll be able to encourage others. Encouragement is "to
inspire; to continue on a chosen course; to impart courage or
confidence." Think back over the past years. Can you remember
practical and specific examples of what you've done that would
illustrate this definition?

You may think of encouragement as praise and reinforcement, but it's also much more than that. Praise is limited; it's a
verbal reward. Praise emphasizes competition, has to be earned
and is often given for being the best. Encouragement, on the
other hand, is freely given. It can involve noticing something in
a person that others take for granted, and affirming something
that others notice but may never think of mentioning. Bruce
Larson shared this experience:

Early one morning, I had to catch a plane from Newark,
New Jersey, to Syracuse, New York, having returned late

the previous night from leading one conference and on my way to another.

I was tired. I had not budgeted my time wisely, and I was totally unprepared for the intense schedule before me. After rising early and hastily eating breakfast, I drove to the airport in a mood that was anything but positive. By the time the plane took off I felt so sorry for myself.

Sitting on the plane with an open notebook in my lap, I prayed, "O God, help me. Let me get something down here that will be useful to your people in Syracuse."

Nothing came. I jotted down phrases at random, feeling worse by the moment, and more and more guilty. Such a situation is a form of a temporary insanity. It denies all that we know about God Himself and His ability to redeem any situation.

About halfway through the brief flight, a stewardess came down the aisle, passing out coffee. All the passengers were men, as women have too much sense to fly at seven o'clock in the morning. As the stewardess approached my seat, I heard her exclaim, "Hey! Someone is wearing English Leather aftershave lotion. I can't resist a man who wears English Leather. Who is it?"

Eagerly, I waved my hand and announced, "It's me."

The stewardess immediately came over and sniffed my cheek while I sat basking in this sudden attention and appreciating the covetous glances from passengers nearby.

All through the remainder of the flight the stewardess and I maintained a cheerful banter each time she passed my seat. She would make some comment, and I would respond gaily. Twenty-five minutes later, when the plane prepared to land, I realized that my temporary insanity had vanished. Despite the fact that I had failed in every way—in budgeting my time, in preparation, in attitude—everything had changed. I was freshly aware that I loved God and that He loved me, in spite of my failure.

What is more, I loved myself and the people around me, and the people who were waiting for me in Syracuse. I was like the Gadarene demoniac after Jesus touched him: clothed, in my right mind and seated at the feet of Jesus. I looked down at the notebook in my lap and found a page full of ideas that could prove useful throughout the weekend.

God, I mused, *how did this happen?* It was then that I realized that someone had entered my life and turned a key. It was just a small key, turned by a very unlikely person. But that simple act of affirmation, that undeserved and unexpected attention, had got me back into the stream.[2]

Encouragement is recognizing your wife as having worth and dignity even though she's imperfect, just like we all are. It means paying attention to her when she's sharing with you. It's listening to her in a way that lets her know she's being listened to. When a wife is encouraged, she does her best and becomes her best.

THE ART OF LISTENING

The road to a person's heart is through the ear. Men and women today have few people who really listen to them. Most of us are often more concerned about what we are going to say when the other person stops talking. This is a violation of Scripture. James tells all of us to "be quick to listen" (Jas. 1:19). Proverbs 18:13 states, "He who answers a matter before he hears [the facts], it is folly and shame to him" (*NASB*).

Many of us have outgoing circuits, but our incoming circuits are clogged. When one woman was asked what her husband could do to bring out the best in her, she said, "Listen— listen without being judgmental or biased; listen and be accepting. Listen just to understand me. Listen instead of criticizing me."

How you listen to your wife also needs to be tailored to her. Men and women have different listening styles, and it helps to understand what these differences are. Women tend to give more responses and feedback while they are listening. Those responses usually mean, "I'm with you" or "I understand" or "I'm connecting with you." They don't always mean, "I agree with you." On the other hand, we men tend not only to say less, but our feedback usually does mean, "I agree with you." Have you run into this difference between the way men and women give feedback? Most of us have. When you're listening to your wife, she may need less feedback from you than you think is necessary. You can't communicate with her like she's a man. Listening quietly to her may lead to a response like, "Thanks for really listening to me. It helps me keep my mind on track when I'm not interrupted."

It's true—poor listening skills have an impact on wives more than many husbands realize. One of the greatest longings of any person is to be listened to. The gift of being a good listener is one of the most healing gifts you can give your wife. Unsolicited advice isn't a healing gift; neither is thinking about what

you are going to say while she is talking . . . and then interrupting or finishing her sentences. Other non-gifts are squelching
her verbal expression of her feelings with reassurances, or taking the conversation off on a tangent that's interesting to you
but has no connection to what your wife has said. You'll read
more about this later.

True encouragement validates that what your wife is doing
or saying makes sense. It's letting her know, "You matter to me."
When you encourage your wife, you respect her as well. You
rephrase negatives to positives by discovering the constructive
elements in situations, such as identifying her strengths and
focusing on her efforts and contributions.

This means that you find something of value to recognize
when everybody else has despaired! Does this take work? You
bet it does. But don't look at it as a chore; it's actually a privi-
lege. Encouragement builds up your wife. It focuses on any resource that can be turned into an asset or strength.

Encouragement also means that you expect the best out of
her. Consider what happened to this young man because his
high school principal expected something more from him.

> I remember vividly the day we had a school assembly.
> Three buddies and I went out behind the school audito-
> rium. We all lit up. We knew we were safe: everyone else
> was in the assembly. And then, who should come around
> the corner but the principal. We were caught red-handed.
> My friends took off in three directions and left me just
> standing there. The principal collared me and dragged
> me down the hall in front of the auditorium just as the
> assembly was letting out. I thought I was going to die.
> Hundreds of kids saw me in this humiliating situation.

He took me into his office and chewed me out royally. It felt as if it lasted forever. Maybe it was only ten or fifteen minutes. I couldn't wait to get out of there. From that time on, I hated this guy. I waited for him to nail my buddies, but he never did. He knew who they were, but he did nothing. One day I saw him in the hall, and I asked why he hadn't gone after them. It wasn't fair that I was singled out.

Instead of giving me an answer there, he grabbed me by the collar, and dragged me back into his office. He sat me down, but the chewing out didn't even last a minute this time. I'll never forget what he said. "I wish your friends the best. I don't know what's going to happen to them, but you could be somebody. I expect more of you than this. You're coasting through life. When are you going to do something with what you've got?" He turned around and walked out. I felt like I had been slapped across the face. He was right; I was coasting. And there is only one direction you can coast—down.

I was a junior at that time. I started working a little bit in my classes and made a new group of friends. My senior year I had an *A* average. I had been getting *C*'s and *D*'s before. I decided I wanted to go to college, but when I applied, I couldn't get in. My grades were too bad in a previous term. My principal wrote a letter of recommendation on my behalf, and in response the university agreed to admit me on a probationary status. I chose the field I did because of this man. He became like a mentor, like a second father to me.

Two years ago I gave the eulogy at his funeral. I'll never forget him. I will always be different because of him. He gave me something to live up to.[3]

We've become skilled as flaw finders in our culture. But encouragement is just the opposite of a deficit-oriented approach. To be an encourager you need to go counter to our culture and not be "conformed to this world." Would your wife say you're more equipped to point out her mistakes, weaknesses or liabilities rather than strengths? Your answer speaks volumes, as one man discovered:

When I married my wife, we both were insecure, and she did everything she could to try to please me. I didn't realize how dominating and uncaring I was toward her. My actions in our early marriage caused her to withdraw even more. I wanted her to be self-assured, to hold her head high and her shoulders back. I wanted her to wear her hair long and be perfect at all times. I wanted her to be feminine and sensual.

The more I wanted her to change, the more withdrawn and insecure she felt. I was causing her to be the opposite of what I wanted her to be. I began to realize the demands I was putting on her, not so much by words but by my body language.

By God's grace, I learned that I must love the woman I married, not the woman of my fantasies. I made a commitment to love Susan for who she is—who God created her to be.

The change came about in a very interesting way. During a trip to Atlanta, I read an article in *Reader's Digest*. I made a copy of it and have kept it in my heart and mind ever since.

It was the story of Johnny Lingo, a man who lived in the South Pacific. The islanders all spoke highly of this man, but when it came time for him to find a wife, the people shook their heads in disbelief. In order to obtain a wife, you paid for her by giving her father cows. Four to six cows was considered a high price. But the woman Johnny Lingo chose was plain, skinny and walked with her shoulders hunched and her head down. She was very hesitant and shy. What surprised everyone was Johnny's offer—he gave eight cows for her! Everyone chuckled about it, since they believed his father-in-law put one over on him.

Several months after the wedding, a visitor from the U.S. came to the Islands to trade and heard the story about Johnny Lingo and his eight-cow wife. Upon meeting Johnny and his wife the visitor was totally taken aback, since this wasn't a shy, plain and hesitant woman but one who was beautiful, poised and confident. The visitor asked about the transformation, and Johnny Lingo's response was very simple, "I wanted an eight-cow woman, and when I paid that for her and treated her in that fashion, she began to believe that she was an eight-cow woman. She discovered she was worth more than any other woman in the islands. And what matters most is what a woman thinks about herself."

This simple story impacted my life. I immediately sent Susan flowers (I had rarely if ever done that before). The message on the card simply said, "To My Eight-Cow Wife." The florist (who was a friend of mine) thought I had lost my mind and questioned if that was really what I wanted to say.

Susan received the flowers with total surprise and bewilderment at the card. When I returned from the trip I told her that I loved her for who she is and that I considered her to be my eight-cow wife, and then I gave her the article to read.

I now look for ways to show her that I am proud of her and how much I appreciate her. An example of this involved a ring. When we became engaged I gave Susan an antique engagement ring that I inherited from a great-great aunt. Susan seemed very pleased and I never thought any more about it. But I had come out cheap, and that's how she felt. After 20 years of marriage she shared with me how she felt about the hand-me-down wedding ring. We had our whole family get involved in learning about diamonds. Susan found one that she liked. It was not the largest stone, nor the most expensive. I would have gladly paid more. I bought it and gave it to her at Christmas. "To my Eight-Cow Wife, with all my love!" But what this did for our relationship is amazing.

First, it changed me! My desires began to change. My desire now is for Susan to be all that God has designed her to be. It is my responsibility as her husband to allow her that freedom.

It also changed her. Susan became free. She learned who she is in Christ. She has gained confidence and self-assurance. She is more aware of her appearance, her clothes, hair and makeup, because she is free to be who she is.

Susan rarely buys clothes for herself. Last year for Christmas I told her this year I would buy her an outfit or some type of clothing each month. This has boosted her confidence in her appearance. She looks great because she wants to!

Susan really is an Eight-Cow Wife of whom I am very proud. We have been married now since 1971.

ENCOURAGEMENT AND ACCEPTANCE GO HAND IN HAND

Time and time again we hear about the positive aspect of an encouraging parent upon a child. I remember hearing an interview one day with Scott Hamilton, who has become a household name in professional ice-skating. During the 1992 Winter Olympics, Scott served as a commentator for the ice-skating events. During his time on TV, he shared about his special relationship with his mother, who died prior to his winning an Olympic gold medal. He said, "The first time I skated in the U.S. Nationals, I fell five times. My mother gave me a big hug and said, 'It's only your first National. It's no big deal.' My mother always let me be me. Three years later I won my first National. She never said 'you can do better' or 'shape up.' She just encouraged me."

A wife shared with me, "My husband is a very supportive person. He believed in what I could do even when I didn't, especially in the early years of marriage. Oh, he gave his opinion and lots of advice, but without being judgmental. He cared about me as a person, not just what I did or could do. In time I felt I could do anything I set out to tackle. But the best thing he ever gave me was his belief in me. He still does."

Encouragement means that you show faith in your wife and her potential. It means that you believe in her without the evidence that she is believable. That's hard for those who think, "I'll believe it when I see it."

Perhaps you have a dream for your wife. You're able to see things that she can't see, such as untapped potential. Have you ever heard of the four-eyed fish? It's an odd-looking creature. I don't think you'd want one mounted on your wall. It's a fish native to the equatorial waters of the Western Atlantic region. Anableps is the technical name of this fish. (Just don't name one of your children Anableps!) It means "those that look upward" because of the unusual eye structure. This unique creature has two-tiered eyes. The upper and lower halves of each eyeball operate independently and have separate corneas and irises. So, if you were to confront one in its natural habitat, you would see him with his upper eyes protruding above the surface of the water. This helps him search for food as well as identify enemies in the air.

Now remember, this fish also has lower eyes. These eyes stay focused in the water in the typical manner of most fish. On one hand the fish navigates in the water like other fish. But they have the advantage of seeing what other fish can't see because of their upper eyes. They see in both worlds. If you were like this, having four eyes, two for seeing what actually is and two for seeing what might be, you would be an unusual encourager![4] How are you doing this with your wife at this time in your life?

John Maxwell, in his book *Be a People Person*, says we need to anticipate that others will do their best. "When working with people I always try to look at them not as they are but as what they can be. By anticipating that the vision will become real, it's easy for me to encourage them as they stretch. Raise your anticipation level, and you raise their achievement level."[5]

Perhaps the best way to describe encouragement is through the example of gardening. I've raised flowers and vegetables for years. Some years were good; others I'd rather forget! At times I've raised tomatoes. There's a right way to raise tomatoes and a wrong way. The right way is to make sure you have good soil with plenty of nutrients. You need water, cultivation and fertilizers in the right amounts. You also need to stake the plant or use round wire cages for them to grow on. They need this support, or their branches will break. Sometimes you need to put up a protective cover and, above all, watch out for insects, especially tomato worms.

After you've done all this you can take several weeks off to do nothing, right? No, you have to care for tomato plants consistently rather than sporadically, or they won't produce a crop.

Giving encouragement is like caring for tomato plants. It takes work—constant, consistent work—for it to be effective.[6] When you're an encourager, you're like a prospector or a deep-sea diver looking for hidden treasure. Every woman has pockets of underdeveloped resources within her. Your task as a husband is to search for these underdeveloped resources in your wife, discover them and then expand them. As you discover the strengths in your wife, you'll begin to focus on them. You'll look at them and care about what you discover. At first what you discover may be rough and imperfect. Talent scouts and scouts for professional sports teams do this all the time. They see undeveloped raw talent and ability, but they have the wisdom to see beyond that. They look into the future and see what can happen if all that potential were cultivated and developed. Do you look at your wife that way?

Encouraging your wife means that you honor and respect her because you believe in her.

I entered sports late in life. I took up racquetball in my early forties. One of the reasons I kept at it was a young pastor who worked with me the first few months. At first, I was a bit discouraged, especially when I noticed the proficiency of some of the younger men. But Tom was patient and excited whenever I did something right. He encouraged me; he believed in my ability; he saw me for what I could become, and that made so much difference. Almost 20 years later, I still played. I gained confidence, and some of those younger guys didn't beat me anymore!

What Encouragement Brings About

You are like the refiner's fire. What you notice and encourage can be refined in a positive way. Any movement that you see headed in a healthy, positive direction needs your attention and reinforcement.[7] You're saying, "Go for it. You can do it!"

One of the character qualities that lend themselves to being an encourager is gentleness. This quality means that when you discover where another person is vulnerable or sensitive, you're not hard, harsh or forceful. When you discover a tender, sensitive place in your wife, you protect it rather then step on it. As you consider ways of encouraging your wife, ask yourself:

- Am I gentle, especially with those sensitive areas?
- Am I treating her the way I would want to be treated?
- Am I building hope in her life?
- Does she feel safe around me with those sensitive areas?

A husband shared with me how he encouraged his wife to take some steps to move forward in her life:

My wife and I were accustomed to living on two average incomes when our first child was born and I began seminary. Both of us went to part-time work in order to adjust to our new family and the demands of school. Our reduced income also necessitated a move to a much less attractive house. In addition, it became necessary for us to be much more thrifty than either one of us had ever experienced. My wife is not naturally given to bargain hunting, coupon shopping or other cost-saving measures. Being naturally a bit of a tightwad, I realized that I needed to encourage change.

To encourage my wife to change her shopping habits, I did several things: (1) I prayed for her to be open to change and that God would show me what to do and say so that she wanted to change; (2) I very tactfully passed on cost-cutting ideas I was aware of or learned about; (3) I held up the virtues of cost cutting and the practices of other thrifty women we both knew, praising her each time she came home with a bargain; (4) I set an example of thriftiness and cost consciousness; (5) I allowed her to change and exhort me in this area as well; (6) I trusted God to change her, because I couldn't do it alone.

The challenge of living on less, especially with school and then a second child, was sometimes intimidating. However, we were still able to tithe to our church and continue to save, even while my wife was out of work following the birth of girl number two. My wife is not proud of her management of the household finances, but I am proud of her, and we both have a deeper appreciation for the way that God blesses those who are good stewards of what He entrusts to them. We've been blessed by freedom from the love of money and things—and by generosity of others in

times of special need. We worked together construc-
tively, and a potential threat to our relationship has
brought us closer together and given us confidence in
facing other challenges.

Perhaps you're like some men I've talked to, or I should say,
men who have talked to me! They say, "Why do I need to be the
one doing all the encouraging? I need it as much as she does, and
I'm starving for some."

"This sounds just like what I've been hearing for years. We
guys have to give, give and give. And if I do more of this, she'll
just expect more!"

"This sounds one-sided to me. Many of us men go through
life starving for some need fulfillment. Why don't you work with
wives to get them to be more caring?"

These are good, honest questions. I have two responses.

First, this is *not* a book directed to women. It's written to encourage men to bring out the best in the women in their lives.
We, as husbands, have a need to grow and develop as encouragers.
In a marriage relationship, we often function as a thermostat.
What we do affects the temperature of that relationship. Most
men were raised in a way that handicapped them emotionally and
made them relationally deficient; and I'm saying that about myself as well. We have much to learn! And we can do better (some
of us have already learned to do better as a marriage partner). But
there are other books and helps for women to read, including the
companion to this volume—*Bringing Out the Best in Your Husband*.
The book you are reading, however, is for men.

Second, as Christians, we don't really have a choice about
whether we encourage others or not. It's not our decision to make.
Scripture states that others will know that we are Christians by

the love we show for one another. One of the ways we reflect this love is by being an encourager. Look at what God's Word tells us to do.

In Acts 18:27, the word "encourage" means "to urge forward or persuade." In 1 Thessalonians 5:11, it means "to stimulate another person to the ordinary duties of life."

Consider the words found in 1 Thessalonians 5:14: "And we earnestly beseech you, brethren, admonish (warn and seriously advise) those who are out of line [the loafers, the disorderly, and the unruly]; encourage the timid and fainthearted, help and give your support to the weak souls, [and] be very patient with everybody [always keeping your temper]" (*AMP*).

Scripture uses a variety of words to describe both our involvement with others as well as the actual relationships. The word "urge" (*parakaleo*) means "to beseech or exhort." It is intended to create an environment of urgency to listen and respond to a directive. It is a mildly active verb. Paul used it in Romans 12:1 and in 1 Corinthians 1:4.

The word "encourage" (*paramutheomai*) means "to console, comfort and cheer up." This process includes elements of understanding, redirecting of thoughts and a general shifting of focus from the negative to the positive. In the context of the verse, it refers to the timid ("fainthearted" in the *KJV*) individual who is discouraged and ready to give up. It's a matter of loaning your faith and hope to the person until her own develops. In what way does your wife need you to loan your faith to her?

The word "help" (*anechomai*) primarily contains the idea of "taking interest in, being devoted to, rendering assistance or holding up spiritually and emotionally." It is not so much an active involvement as a passive approach. It suggests the idea of coming alongside a person and supporting him. In the context of 1 Thessalonians 5:14, it seems to refer to those who are incapable of helping themselves. In what way does your wife need this kind of help at this time?

First Thessalonians 5:11 states, "Therefore encourage one another and build each other up, just as in fact you are doing." Hebrews 3:13 states that we are to "encourage one another daily." In the setting of this verse, encouragement is associated with protecting the believer from callousness. Hebrews 10:25 says, "Let us not give up meeting together . . . but let us encourage one another." This time, the word means to keep someone on his feet who, if left to himself, would collapse. Your encouragement serves like the concrete pilings of a structural support. In what way does your wife need this kind of support at this time? One of my favorite verses is Proverbs 12:25: "Anxiety in a man's heart weighs it down, but a good word makes it glad" (*NASB*).

The Word of God is clear about what we're to do. To be a consistent encourager we need to reflect the character qualities of 1 Corinthians 13. Here they are, amplified in a unique way:

- *Patient* (you are tolerant of frailties, imperfections and shortcomings in your wife)
- *Kind* (you are tender and thoughtful toward your wife)
- *Not jealous* (of genuine friendships with others or of the special gifts and talents of your wife)
- *Not boastful* (about personal appearance or achievements in an attempt to compete with your wife)
- *Not arrogant* (you are not disdainful of your wife's looks or achievements; you do not belittle your wife)
- *Not rude* (you are not inconsiderate of your wife's needs or feelings)

- *Not insistent on your own way* (you are willing to compromise, to consider your wife's needs and interests)
- *Not irritable* (you do not snap at your wife; you are approachable)
- *Not resentful* (you do not hold grudges; you are forgiving)
- *Not rejoicing in wrong* (you do not delight in your wife's misfortunes; you do not keep score or tally perceived wrongs)
- *Rejoicing in right* (you are truthful; you do not try to conceal things from your wife)
- *Bearing all things* (you support your wife in times of struggle)
- *Believing all things* (you consider what your wife has said before responding)
- *Hoping in all things* (you do not wallow in pessimism about your relationship; you keep a positive attitude)
- *Enduring in all things* (you do not give in to pressures of life; you are willing to stand by your wife when she's having personal struggles)[8]

If you want a wife of character, who responds to you, follow the directives in this Scripture passage. The classic Proverbs 31:10-11 Scripture passage reveals a key element of why the Proverbs woman is the way she is. The *New International Version* says, "Her husband has full confidence in her." The *New American Standard* version says, "The heart of her husband trusts in her." Perhaps *THE MESSAGE* version sums it up best:

A good woman is hard to find, and worth far more than diamonds. Her husband treats her without reserve, and never has reason to regret it. Never spiteful, she treats him generously all her life long.

What is in your heart for your wife today?

DISCOVER THE ENCOURAGER IN YOU

1. What is more typical of you—to tell your wife what she does wrong or what she does right? What behaviors bring out the worst response in you?

2. Think about various times when you know your words have influenced your wife's self-esteem, either positively or negatively. Try to remember what you noticed about her then—the way she dressed, the way she wore her hair and makeup, the way she carried herself. What conclusions can you draw from this about you as a catalyst for positive or negative change?

3. The word "encourage" (*paramutheomai*) means "to console, comfort and cheer up." In the context of 1 Thessalonians 5:14, it refers to the timid ("fainthearted" in the *KJV*) individual who is discouraged and ready to give up. It's a matter of loaning your faith and hope to another person. In what way does your wife need you to loan your faith to her right now?

4. Review the bulleted list of 15 character qualities that define love (from 1 Corinthians 13:4-7). Choose the characteristic that is most problematic in your relationship with your wife. Ask God to create in you the character quality you would most like to develop. Consider what kind of speech or actions would reflect that quality to your wife. (This will be a spiritual exercise to do over again and again as God shows you new ways to love and encourage your wife and empowers you to do it.)

5. How does the Proverbs 31:10-11 passage describe the way you view your wife? If it does not describe what's in your heart for your wife right now, what types of behaviors in you, gleaned from this chapter, could encourage her to become more like a woman who is "worth far more than diamonds"?

2

Husbands
Speak Out

ONE OF THE BENEFITS OF WRITING THIS BOOK IS THE DISCOVERY OF WHAT MEN ARE DOING TO BRING OUT THE BEST IN THEIR WIVES. It's encouraging to hear about the creativity, candor and commitment on the part of so many men who are making a difference in their marriages. As you read these accounts, some of which are bottom line while others are quite expansive, ask yourself two questions: (1) *Am I doing something like this in my marriage?* (2) *Would I be willing to do this?* You may discover some new ways to respond, or you may end up feeling like you're doing a pretty good job already.

> When I understand my wife's feelings and emotions and support her by doing what she likes, she responds to me with gladness. Usually it takes a long time to figure out exactly what she wants, but once I realize it and act on it, she is very pleased. I show her my respect and encouragement through my actions.

> As a husband, I try to encourage my wife from time to time even though she often makes mistakes.

> I encourage her by spending time with her, rather than with a group of people or other people.

No question—die to self by living to meet her needs. Communicate better—listening is good, but attending alertly is better.

I need to take care of my wife's family (her aging parents) and her safety issues (doors locked/cars tuned up). I also need to keep her love-language gas tank full (quality time and words of affirmation).

Complimenting her continuously and genuinely is critical. I try to know her and know all the things she expects me to take care of. If I neglect to do things she expects me to do, I bring out the worst in her. I need to communicate everything with her. When she knows everything, she is very supportive; but when she feels left out she gets frustrated.

I demonstrate good leadership.

I don't attempt to make her be a certain way that she is not made to be. For example, she can't cook, so I don't pressure her to be a better cook.

I usually give her something, such as letters or flowers, to let her know how I value and appreciate her and her sacrifice for our family.

First of all, my wife and I have always tried to encourage the other to pursue individual passions in addition to our shared goals and dreams (kids, house, family). So, in the midst of all the pressures of getting married, having kids, buying a house, embarking on our careers and keeping the finances in order, I try to encourage my wife to do things that feed her soul. For my wife, that means taking dance classes on her own, doing creative projects with friends, and taking time to play the guitar and sing. It unleashes such incredible talent in her when she is simply free to dream a bit, even when there is limited time for both of us to do that. When she doesn't get time to do these small things, she starts to get into the grind of the day-to-day, and she soon starts to forget about those passions. I think the key for me has been simply to encourage her in these pursuits, and then I have to make the time for her to pursue these things outside of her time at home (even if it's only a couple hours a week). I have found that this gives her great joy and passion after long days at home with the kids. It charges her up and, as a result, she has reciprocated and allowed me time to do the same!

Second, my wife loves it when our house is clean, as many wives do (especially when they have three young children messing it up all day long!). And, to be honest, most days I don't worry too much about a clean house. I never understood why this was so important for women until I began to actively try to help my wife in this way. Now, I'm no Martha Stewart, but after many discussions about helping out around the house, I now do the dishes more often, take out the trash, and generally do more things around the house (it becomes habitual after a while). Sometimes when she's out working, I'll have the kids help me clean up the house and we'll get everything smelling wonderful. My wife's reaction to these small acts is beyond what I ever imagined they could be. She'll come home and, instead of immediately starting to clean the house, she'll stop and relax after a long day. In a busy week, these moments are important.

Finally, the most important thing I can do for my wife is to make time to be with her myself. It is very difficult in some stages of marriage to simply be together and talk and make that emotional connection. So it is crucial for us to set aside time every week just to talk and hear from each other. To be honest, for me it can be the easiest thing to forget about doing this some weeks. So when I set up a date night and call up a baby-sitter so that she and I can go out and sit down together for a couple of hours, that time is invaluable to our marriage. It brings out our best attitudes over the week following.

I encourage and praise her for all she does to support and nourish the family. I reinforce how important her role is as a stay-at-home mom. I provide as much support as possible with her tasks and with down time. I pray and fast the first Wednesday every month for her.

I talk to her and give her my full and undivided attention. I affirm her and the beauty she brings into our home. I do what she wants me to do—shop, spend time with her family, prepare for meals, clean-up, do laundry, vacuum the floors, plant roses.

I try to really listen to my wife without trying to "fix" the problems. I give her a listening ear. She is the happiest when I listen carefully and let her know that she has my full attention. I bring out the best in my wife when I just spend time with her, either by taking her out for coffee or to dinner or by planning something out of the ordinary "rat-race" of our lives.

She is very happy when I pitch in by doing the dishes (without having to be asked), or when I clean up my side of the bedroom, or when I show that I care about her sense of order and detail. If it were up to me, our home would look like an army warehouse, so I tell her how much I appreciate her design and decoration in the house, and I try to do concrete things to preserve and support what she has done.

My wife appreciates it when I treat her as a valuable friend whose discernment and wisdom I really need. Instead of invalidating her observations, I take them seriously, because I've learned in 25 years of marriage that if I don't take seriously her discernment about people and situations, I get into more trouble, grief and pain than is necessary!

She loves receiving gifts, so I give her little notes, flowers at unexpected times, and phone calls just to say, "I love you; you're the best part of me." She is excellent one on one. I try to put her in individual situations so she can use her strengths, and I constantly pray for God to use her, build her, encourage her and show her who she is in Him.

I help with the laundry, make dinner, and talk to her about her day at work. I listen, but I don't make suggestions on how I would try to fix something.

I help her with her chores *without being asked*. I constantly remind her how beautiful she is and how much I love her. I spend time with her—a *lot* of time.

To encourage her on a day-to-day basis, I do my part around the house and help the kids with homework or do activities with the kids. For a special time—either a special occasion or surprise—I plan a weekend getaway for just the two of us.

I encourage her by being the most Christian man I can be and leading the household through Christ. I try to set a good example for my kids. As I lift myself up and grow in Christ, so does my wife.

My wife just told me that what really turns her on is when I'm a good father and grandfather. We spend quality time together, and I try to do anything I can to make her feel important.

I give her words of affirmation. I compliment her attributes and daily activities and try to pay close attention to her everyday needs. I try to be close with her, clear in my communication and transparent. I pray with her and encourage her.

I make her favorite dinner as a surprise. I leave her sticky notes with messages about what a wonderful wife and mother she is. I arrange a shopping date with her friends for her to enjoy. I give the kids a bath without her asking. I fold the laundry when she walks away from it to tend to another chore.

I show her affection by hugging her and telling her that I love her. She likes affirmation ("nice dress," "you look good," "thanks for your support").

I encourage her by being present and actively listening without giving advice—which is a great way to validate her emotions. When she's stressed, I jump in and do extra chores. A clean kitchen and laundry room are a delight to her.

I encourage her and support her. I actively listen to her, especially at the end of the day . . . it does wonders.

I praise her.

I make sure that when she asks me to do a project, I complete it *as she would*. I make sure to double-check all projects.

I try to do something for her before she asks for it to be done. I talk with her and review her day—what went well; what needs to change.

I talk with her about how her day went at work, asking details as she shares to show my interest in her work and her relationships at the office.

I compliment her about what she is good at. This is hard for me to do, and it takes a lot of work on my part.

I remember our wedding date on a monthly basis! We have lunch together. I give her neck rubs and back rubs.

I allow my wife to be who she wants to be. I encourage her by allowing her to be creative and reach her potential. I support her mentally and verbally to help make her feel important.

When my wife tells me that something is broken at home, or that something is wrong with the car, or that we need to get insurance for the family, I respond. She feels secure and safe, because I act and minister to her concerns.

I frequently and consistently offer her encouragement and praise. I do this in a variety of ways: verbally, through Post-It notes (often in surprise locations—vanity mirror, in a book she is reading, on her laptop screen), and by sending text messages and emails. I try to mix it up and be creative, spontaneous and surprising. Romance her.

I try to do housework without being asked. She's a clean freak, and I'm not. She feels loved when I help out in that area.

I bring out the good within her. In our marriage we struggle at times, but in that struggle I turn to God for prayer and answers. She tends to follow my lead when she sees me do that.

I give my wife one day (or weekend) each month as a "you name it—I'll do it!" day. This includes doing projects, going on special visits, and doing the shopping. Every Friday night is date night, so I take her out to dinner or cook dinner for her.

I like to bring laughter, joy and love to our family. I try to find something she enjoys and dwell on it. I do things for her without being asked and tell her that I love her and enjoy life with her.

First, I encourage her by doing things to show her I love her. I make sure the house is cleaned up and that messes the kids and I make are minimal. Second, I tell her I love her. Always being encouraging.

I take her on a date about once a week—just the two of us. I try to get home right after work to relieve her of her mom duties as soon as possible. Every evening, I take time to sit down one on one and talk through her day.

I bring out the best in her by saying "yes, dear" to whatever she asks.

I show her that she has my full commitment—my full support. I try to be a good listener, work as a team player and have a full commitment in family things—church, kids, and so on. I feel that the greatest commitment as a husband is to show love and respect for her. We spend time together, but I also give her time for privacy. We pray together.

I've learned the following: (1) do not aim any jokes her way, (2) do not try to wash your own clothes, (3) do not ever complain about her not taking care of a certain item, (4) do not ever mention weight, dress or hair in a constructive manner.

I communicate and listen (initiate conversation) and try to ask more open-ended questions. I acknowledge her role and accomplishments and help out with the kids. I try to be quiet and rely on prompts to communicate.

My wife is naturally negative, so I compliment her whenever she has a positive attitude.

I ask her what her needs are and how I can fulfill them. I act on this information and make fulfilling these needs a priority.

I want her to feel the freedom to make her own choices in life. She is an awesome and godly woman, and I don't want to be the bump in the road that takes her off course. If I have any insights on how she can overcome her weaknesses, I share these in love. I need to do more things in the home to give her time for herself.

My love language is to help—do the laundry, wash the dishes, clean the kitchen, take care of the cars. I know that sometimes I do too much, but it gives my wife the freedom to do her tasks, send emails, go shopping, take outings with friends, or study for women's ministry. In what I'm doing, I'm supporting her role as a person, expanded beyond just mother, cook and chauffeur. Also, I listen to all the details of her conversation. She's smart and intuitive, especially with the kids. I know that words of affirmation are important to her, so I try to be spontaneous, telling her that she's beautiful, that I've missed her, that I want her. Her family is important to her as well, so we always make time for them and are generous toward them.

I encourage her in the areas of life where she feels inadequate. In many ways she still feels like a little girl, although she never acts like one.

I listen—and *think twice* before I respond.

I try to listen to her and let issues go by that are not worth arguing over. I support her in times when others come against her.

I take her out for an evening of dining and entertainment. We talk about her interests, her associations and her endeavors.

I don't forget anniversaries, birthdays, Christmas—and I speak silently.

I spend time on my knees before the Lord, praying and studying the Word (see Psalm 119:11), which changes me.

I encourage my wife in her endeavors and help her when she asks. I also compliment her.

I listen to her, show interest in what she's saying, and spend time with her.

I always encourage her in her endeavors, especially when she has self-doubts about her activities. I share in all the household work.

We have committed to have one date night each week since we married, and I have followed through. It's just the two of us—and we have seven children.

I tell her how much I enjoy her company over all else—sports and other hobbies. I go and do the things she likes to do (like shopping).

I ask, "Do you have anything for me to do?" and "Have you been okay today?"

I think it's important to be flexible. Don't have your own agenda—give and take. Be respectful and complimentary, and help her with anything she needs.

I try to treat her like a queen. I tell her she is beautiful and give her tools so she can feel beautiful. I tell her the things she did well and the things I like about her. I appreciate her artistic, creative bent, even though it may not be interesting to me. I read the Bible with her and have Bible study time with her, and we pray together.

My goal is to love her in the same way Jesus loves His bride. There is nothing that I would withhold from her that I could give or that would lessen her radiance. I respect her for all of her God-given talents. I tell her often how much I appreciate her. I trust her in every aspect of our relationship. I try to be a good listener and am learning not to try to fix her problems—it's more about letting her vent and work through them than it is about me solving them. We laugh together—a lot. I hold her.

I open doors for her. I help her with her coat and with her seat and all those other "old-fashioned" things that previous generations (who usually stayed married longer) chose to do. It may be noteworthy to mention that my wife allows me to do those things for her and appreciates them—so the relationship of these actions is in sync with our love. I am trying to further develop my sense of good timing for communication. I am trying to be more aware of my facial expressions and body language that she reads *so* well. I am conscious that I may be sending the wrong message or a message that I did not intend to display as I think through things. I am alert to our differences on parenting (mom kinds of love vs. dad kinds of love). I say all these things not as bragging on myself, but as an acknowledgment that her "bringing out the best" is somewhat reliant on my "giving her the best."

I have found that praying for my wife makes a difference—whether in her presence or on my own. My wife asks me to pray for her in certain ways—when she has some challenges she is working through or when she has certain needs. Just a crazy example: My wife and a neighbor have both struggled with weight at times, and so they walk (and talk) together. But unknown to them, I started praying for them—for their health, friendship and that God would honor their efforts to care for their bodies. Both had struggled with losing weight (her weight has never been an issue for me—but it was for her), but they began to lose weight. So I casually told my wife that I had been praying for them. Now whenever they walk for that purpose, they ask me to pray for them! (By the way, there is no guarantee for this weight-loss plan!) I also try to compliment my wife, whether it is her dress, her food, the way she cares for our family, the mother that she is, her care of our home, the character of her life, or whatever. These are just a couple of quick ways that I have found in our love relationship to show her how much she really means to me. These things cause her to light up, they encourage her, and I believe they bring out the best in her.

Recently, I have been convicted by the Holy Spirit to put my wife ahead of my job, where she should have been all of our marriage. That has made a remarkable change in our relationship. This change has made me feel much more secure in my marriage, which in turn has made my wife more willing to "fill my love bank" as I fill hers. Being more secure has opened the lines of communication. I now understand that she only wants what is best for me, and I only want what is best for her. Knowing this one fact has helped defuse many arguments and made it much easier for us to honestly communicate our feelings to one another. We also try to have a weekend getaway about once a quarter. Nothing fancy, just time to focus on us.

Communication. I take time to be with her.

I try to live my life with Ephesians 5:25 and 1 Peter 3:7 in view: "Husbands, love your wives, just as Christ loved the church and gave himself up for her. . . . Husbands, in the same way be considerate as you live with your wives, and treat them with respect as the weaker partner and as heirs with you of the gracious gift of life, so that nothing will hinder your prayers." I know that Psalm 23:3, "he restores my soul," outlines that my life is not for me, but for Him is a start. Then, longing to finish and to hear "well done" by both God and my wife, I do my best to surrender my all to Christ. When that occurs, I'm blessed to have a wife that responds to godly behavior in me, and not only returns godly behavior but also outgives me.

Before we married, I read Judson Swihart's book *How Do You Say, "I Love You"?* and learned about love languages. I bring out the best in her by investing love in her life in languages that she understands. (In her case, "spending time together" and "saying it with words.") I also show her constant appreciation for her love and dedication to our family. I think I bring out the best in her and make it easier for her to do her job of respecting and submitting to me when I love her as Christ loved the Church, and I am willing to give myself to her.

I pray for my wife in the mornings before we go to work and at night before we go to sleep. We take care of our grandchildren three days a week, and I help prepare meals for them. Also, on days that I have off, I fix meals and help clean the house. I encourage her in her teaching of ladies' Bible studies at the church we attend. I try to remember to tell her every day that I love her and that I appreciate her and what she does to help me do the things that I need to do.

I simply work to be her greatest cheerleader. I encourage her in her new ventures and in opportunities to use her God-given talents and gifts. I let her know on a daily basis how important she is in my life and that I'm more in love with her than ever. I constantly tell her how beautiful she is—both physically and in her heart. I make sure that she knows that we are in this until "death do us part"—that we will survive any trials that life throws at us because we're in this together.

I affirm my love for her daily and tell her how beautiful she is. I demonstrate unconditional love to the best of my ability. I praise her for being such a godly woman and tell her how fortunate I am to be married to her. I stress that we are on the same team and that our teamwork is critical to having a fulfilled life. I could write a book about how intelligent my wife is and how talented she is. She is a Proverbs 31 wife and mother. I love her.

I encourage my wife in several ways. First, I try to support her interests as much as possible. She does so much for our family. I always make myself available so she can participate in activities outside the family that help revitalize her. Second, I help around the house as much as I can (doing dishes, laundry, cleaning, helping with the kids) so she doesn't have the entire burden. Third, we always support each other as parents, even when we disagree on something. Fourth, I try my best just to love and honor her as my wife 100 percent of the time.

I try to actively listen to her. I champion the activities she is passionate about. I thank God for her daily in her presence. I express appreciation for all she does. I scratch her back each night as we are falling asleep, which is her favorite form of touch. I make her laugh. We have fun together. I bring her coffee in bed when she wakes each morning. I read a portion of Scripture and pray with her each day. We share mutual interests.

I think of ways to encourage her and then verbalize them. I may come into the room and "breathe in" out loud—as when you see something that is *awesome*—and I let her know she is. I may write her an email just saying how special she is. I appreciate her laughter and the way she loves the Lord.

I cherish her. I make it a point to understand what is most important to her, and I let her know through my words, actions and prayers that I will do whatever I can do to support her in those things. This often requires sacrifice, patience and humility. However, I don't do this to bring out the best in her but to demonstrate my love and bring out the best in me.

I constantly praise her both in private and in public, giving specific praise for her character and her skills, gifts and accomplishments. Those who have known me for 20 or 30 years have never heard me speak a critical word about her. Long-term, this may be one of the most specific strengths of our marriage. Meanwhile, my wife blooms in the garden of praise; she feels safe, sheltered and valued.

I consciously try to encourage and build up my wife's confidence, emphasizing her abilities and relationship skills. I also try to remove impediments to her by helping with meal preparation and, on occasion, cooking, cleaning, picking up our home, vacuuming and running errands—plus my "honey-do" list. Fortunately, I work at home. My wife is part of the women's leadership team at our church, is a trainer for table leaders for each session of Radiance (a woman's Bible study), and does premarital mentoring with me. She continues to grow in the Lord despite being an above-the-knee amputee and dealing with other health issues.

TWENTY WAYS TO BRING OUT THE BEST IN YOUR WIFE

I received the following list from one husband on how he brings out the best in his wife:

1. I serve the Lord with all my soul, heart, mind and strength and let God bring out the best in me.
2. I obey Scripture regarding my wife.
3. I tell her I love her (not as a foreplay audible).
4. I listen to her (even when I have to push the record button during a play-off overtime).

5. I love her even when she does not "deserve it."
6. I compliment her on her beauty, clothes, cooking, spirituality and marital "performance."
7. I give her flowers regularly (and not the cheesy ones).
8. I am honest with her at all times (but I avoid suicidal opinions).
9. I tell her I think of no other woman (i.e., no alternate fantasies).
10. I pray with her.
11. I don't insist on sex when she's tired.
12. I maintain a godly, peaceful atmosphere in our home.
13. I keep her laughing (self-deprecating humor works best).
14. When she's wrong, I have the character to admit it.
15. I remind her that opposites attract, and that I'm the smart one.
16. Date night is Friday night, and I don't flake out.
17. Rubdowns are good (and so is whatever happens after).
18. I get her something hot (wintertime) or cold (summertime).
19. I avoid criticizing her (an effective antidepressant).
20. "Sex starts in the kitchen," a cold (floor) metaphor for me, but I try to maintain the romance (very important).
21. Extra: I got turned on just making this list!

Now that you've read what others have said, what's your reaction? Did you gather some new ideas? Was it overwhelming? Were you encouraged or discouraged? If you had to summarize what you read or list the top six ideas, what would you say? Perhaps you're wondering, "Is all this worth it?" "Will it really help?" or "Our marriage is in too bad a shape at this point; I've given up." Well, it's never too late.

Listen to the story of a couple of friends of mine. At one point it was too late, but redemption occurred.

Here is Jim's story:

I wondered why I was asked to give my testimony, and then I realized that the pastor knew that Marie and I were divorced and then remarried. I first thought the reason they asked me to share was that out of all the people in the congregation I had done the worst job the first time around in marriage. But when we had the *Forty Days of Purpose*, one of the things I remembered from the book was when it talked about life as a metaphor. What immediately flashed in my mind is that it's a battle and a struggle. And it's always been a battle and a struggle for me.

Marie and I were both living in Los Angeles in what most people would call the ghetto. We met when my mother worked with Marie's aunt. They wanted me to take her to her prom and I said no because I didn't have any fun at mine. Then I saw her picture and said yes. Eventually, in 1966, we were married.

I always believed in God, but I never let Him into my life, and I always tried to fight all the battles and struggles myself. I was a basketball coach and was focused on winning, winning and winning. That's all I thought about. I brought all those struggles home and dumped them on her. Even though I was a leader at work, I really wasn't a leader at home. I just didn't know how to lead my family.

We were married 23 years before we got divorced in 1989, basically because I was such a poor leader. I did not give my wife the things she needed. I really didn't know exactly what those things were. We went through with the divorce and Marie went to Mexico City to study. I was a Christian at the time, but I wasn't walking with the Lord. But I prayed and asked Him to take over because I loved my wife and my family and I did not want this situation. God was faithful to me and restored my marriage a year later. We were only divorced for one year.

I think the major things I have learned are that I can trust the Lord to fight my battles and that He will lead me if I give Him that opportunity. I think the major change in my life is that I am more of a spiritual leader in my home. I think I support my wife more now.

I know that women need to be loved, supported and cherished. As men, that's really the role God has given us—and He sets an example when He loves, supports and cherishes His church. I'm trying to do a better job on that. I don't always do it, but the more that I can be in the Bible and listen to God speaking to me— because that's where He's speaking to me—and the more I can rely on Him, the more I can focus on my wife's positive gifts rather than on her negative traits and on trying to change her.

You see, that's what coaches do—we work on changing negative behavior so that we can get players to do the positive things so that we can be successful. But I know I shouldn't carry that home—and that's what I did for years.

Marie is a very intelligent, compassionate, loving and beautiful woman. We are very different. Last night, for example, she was reading her welding book and I was watching the De La Hoya fight. But we are meant to be together. The Scripture that I have relied on is 1 Peter 3:7, which says, "Live with your wives in an understanding way . . . show them respect" (*NCV*).

Here is Marie's response:

I really like the cherish part; Jim was always a hardworking, responsible man. I never had to worry about any of the material things in our life, but I felt way down on his list of priorities. It seemed like basketball was number one, two and three. He was very critical of me—whether it be my dress, my hair or the smudge on the table. It didn't seem like I could do anything well, and the irony of it was that other people thought I did many things well. But none of that sank into my heart, because Jim was the one I wanted to please. My sell-out to the Lord has made such an incredible difference in our lives. Now Jim's self-esteem was very wrapped up in what he thought of me.

My family had died. I was a young woman trying to raise a family—and without a foundation in the Lord. In fact, in our early marriage I was an atheist because of a lot of things that had happened to me. I was needy, and Jim wasn't able to show me the love he actually had for me.

I started to build up sadness and deep depression over the years, and after 23 years, I thought, *I can't go on any longer like this*. But crying out to the Lord is an amazing thing. It wasn't an overnight change, but it turns out a church I was attending needed a singer and guitarist and I was pushed into the role. That's where I found out God was real, that Jesus Christ had died for my sins and that He was there for me.

Jim and I reaching out to the Lord has made such an incredible difference in our lives. Now Jim reads the Word faithfully, and I can see that he's devoted his life to God's plan. This has been a benefit to me and our family, because God's plan is that we be united. That has enriched our relationship.

Jim is now my biggest supporter. He helped me overcome my fear of going to school, so at the age of 44, I went to college, got a bachelor's, master's, two teaching credentials and two administrative credentials—when I thought I never could pass one college class.

And then last May Jim pushed me into doing a concert that was a magical experience—at an auditorium with more than 600 people in attendance. I have found that I can rely upon my husband not just for material things, but for spiritual strength and for emotional support. Now he enumerates my strengths to me and to other people. He also helps me with my weaknesses, as a spouse should do, and in an uncritical way.

It's an amazing thing. In a short sentence: There is always hope in the Lord.

DISCOVER THE ENCOURAGER IN YOU

1. As you read the men's comments in this chapter, what was your response?

2. What did you learn about encouragement? What one thing stood out to you?

3. Several of the men not only told how they encourage their wives, but they also told some of the positive effects their encouragement had on their wives. What did their stories inspire in you?

4. What are you doing to encourage your wife right now?

5. What will you do differently to encourage her in the future?

3

Wives
Speak Out

IN POPULAR CULTURE, HUSBANDS ARE OFTEN THE BRUNT OF JOKES, which often revolve around the belief that they don't always know how to respond to their wives or they don't understand them.

I once picked up a small book in a store with the title *What Men Understand About Women.* To my surprise, I discovered every page was blank. The message was all too apparent. But was it true? Unfortunately, in many cases, it is the truth. Having spent 40 years counseling couples and conducting marriage seminars throughout the country, I've found that women are much more concerned about learning about marriage and the man they married. They want to grow in their understanding. There is also evidence in the fact that 85 percent of Christian books are purchased and read by women. If men would study women, and their wives in particular, with the same intensity they put forth (at least some of them) in getting an education, developing their athletic ability or becoming proficient in their vocation, marriage counselors would start going out of business!

It helps a man when he is given some direction. That's what this chapter is about. I look to surveys for a lot of my information; but to discover how a man can really bring out the best in his wife, I needed feedback from wives, and lots of them. So I asked a few questions and also looked to others' surveys, which also asked questions of women. And we found answers.

Scores of wives shared what their husbands did to bring out the best in them. It helps a man to find out what other men are doing so that he can think about it for as long as he wants, decide what he wants to do and then follow through. But remember that each wife is unique, and every husband will need to discover what works best for his own wife.

Encouraging Your Spouse

Here are the responses that can shed some light on what you might do to encourage your wife:

He communicates his love and appreciation for me daily—with email, texts, words, body language and physical touch. He shows me love physically on a regular basis: hugs, kisses, loving touches. He only uses kind, gentle words, because he knows I'm sensitive and he knows that words are my love language.

He supports me emotionally—even when he thinks I'm wrong. He always backs me up. He encourages me in all my endeavors and supports my decisions. He's there to catch me when I fall.

He compliments me, especially in front of others. He does things that show he has listened and paid attention to what I have said. He helps me when I ask. He's loyal and trustworthy. He gives me backrubs. He stands up for me and spends time with me.

My husband encourages me to be creative and to have hobbies and special friends to do them with. He never minds when I spend money on myself to buy nice clothes (maybe because I don't do it very often).

He will take the time to stop and really listen to me and support my thoughts and feelings. He acknowledges and appreciates what I do for him. He compliments me and is impulsively demonstrative when I least expect it.

He really listens and responds to what I am saying. He doesn't try to fix it; he just listens and says things like, "I understand how you would feel that way" or "You are so right." He tells me he still thinks I'm beautiful and will say to me, "Good meal, babe."

What helps is his being a listener *at all times*. He is a good listener because he gives verbal affirmation—he praises and acknowledges my strengths as well as my weaknesses in a positive tone. He spends time with me— trips, coffee time, walks, date night.

When he is thoughtful of me, I'm encouraged. I don't feel that I'm in this family alone when he does his part by working and helping around the house and with the children. When he does these things, my attitude changes and I'm different.

He encourages me to set and follow goals. He gives constructive criticism in a loving way for areas I need to improve, and he likewise allows me to give him my thoughts on areas he needs improvement as a husband/father/son. He understands that staying home with two children under four years old is hard work. He knows exactly when my patience is running on low and keeps the kids to give me a break.

He is patient with me. I'm very emotional, and if I go off on something or about someone, he listens patiently. He lets me get it out of my system. Then, later that day (or even a few days later) after I've come to my senses about that topic, I'm more able to listen to his wisdom and discuss the issue rationally. He doesn't meet me with condemnation when I'm emotional or passionate about something. He quietly leads me to a more forgiving heart.

He is funny. He can change my mood and lighten me up by helping me to see the humor in a situation. He leaves me notes around the house to tell me he loves me. He calls me during the day for no reason but to say he is thinking of me. He says nice things about me in front of our friends.

He stays calm even when I am at my worst. Sometimes even I think I'm being unreasonable, but I can't stop myself until I see how calm he stays. He provides stability.

I feel encouraged when he says he appreciates all the things I do for our family and our home.

When he does things to show me that he loves me—holds me, rubs my neck and shoulders, shares deep personal things—I feel safe.

My husband supports my desires to serve and use my spiritual gifts, even when it requires a sacrifice.

He recognizes my need for time alone and my need for time with my girlfriends.

He always tells me he loves me and kisses me frequently. He tells me how beautiful I am even when I don't feel that I am. I need that.

He listens *without trying to fix things* for me. He makes me feel loved by wanting to spend time with me—whether it is traveling, camping, or something else.

He encourages me in pursuits that make me a better person and closer to God. He never criticizes me. He primarily encourages me and thinks things through before saying anything to me.

His being positive and being a Christian man and husband, in spirit and in action, sets a tone for our family. Being nice to people.

He lets me know clearly and lovingly what he wants and needs from me. I don't have to second guess or read into what he is saying.

He speaks respectfully to me and doesn't nag when I need to change something.

He is a great support to me when we care for our three young grandchildren three evenings a week. He fixes more than his share of meals, does housecleaning and plays board games with them. He also encourages me in my leading a ladies' Bible study.

My gift is teaching and speaking, and he encourages me to take advantage of opportunities and assures me the Lord is using me in this way. He reviews my talks and is honest if they don't make sense. He takes up the slack at home if I need more time. He's my biggest fan.

My husband pampers me, supports me emotionally, serves me and believes in me. His motivation in all of this is to be the leader in our home—always pointing us to Christ.

He really listens and tries to implement something I've said into an actual scenario. I feel at times that it would be easy for him to brush me off and my suggestions, but he doesn't.

He encourages me to share my opinion, which I don't volunteer. He draws me out.

He listens to me and validates me.

He shows how proud he is of me by complimenting me on my appearance or an accomplishment.

He brings out the best in me when he praises me for my accomplishments as a good, loving stepmother and mother. He acknowledges he could not do what I do—being a stay-at-home mother of three young children.

He supports me 100 percent in my endeavors. Throughout my four-and-a-half years in seminary, my husband worked crummy jobs with terrible hours so he could stay with our son. He's listened to my frustrations about being a young woman in ministry, and he's always been my cheerleader. And he's done all of this while also attending school and being shipped overseas twice in the military.

He forgives me immediately when I'm not at my best or when I'm being unreasonable. He supports me in my dreams and surprises me daily by doing household chores (does dishes, makes coffee, feeds cats) or by fixing me breakfast when I'm under pressure. He tells me I am his one and only and that I am beautiful! He listens to me without trying to "fix" it. All this makes me feel special.

He affirms the things I do and am interested in. He makes me want to do better and be better without pressure. I end up wanting to do well.

He encourages me and supports my attending women's Bible study, which keeps me centered. That affects our relationship.

At present, our children are both out of the house (we have a 21-year-old in college and an 18-year-old in the Navy). My husband helps our children understand that I am not trying to control their lives; I only need to hear their voices and small talk. Their voices, he tells them, are helping me cope with the separation a mother must endure as her children grow into independent adults.

My husband is a wonderful listener. He has learned over the years that the way I process problems is by "fleshing them out" out loud—or talking them through. It helps just to have his undivided attention, and then the solution will come to me. I don't necessarily need the problem solved; I just need an ear.

He notices and confirms that what I do routinely is important for him and our family. I don't need to hear this every day, but it is nice for him to notice and affirm the small things that I do over and over again. After years and years of marriage, my husband is great at complimenting my looks and liking the way I look. My husband does not belittle, put me down or say hurtful things to others about me. He is good about saying nice things about me in front of other people.

My husband is an energizer bunny, always moving. When he actually stops to hear what I have to say—and really stops—he really listens. I'm encouraged when he thinks ahead of me and finds something to help me out, like emptying the dishwasher, folding clothes or taking any kind of pressure off my plate. This takes my reactions down and calms me.

He makes me feel that I matter—that I'm special—when he places time with me above job, friends or chores. He encourages me when he is aware of my need to have one-on-one time with him because I need to talk, cuddle or just play. When I feel validated, I, in return, want to please him and help him in all things. When I feel left out, I close off and he does not get my best.

It works best when he listens to me and lets me get out all that I want to say. I want to complete all the details and then get his input. That's ideal. However, realistically, that is very hard for him. He wants to jump in, fix and guess at the conclusion. He gets impatient, doesn't want to hear the details, and wants me to get to the point . . . which is irritating. To bring out the best in me requires his concerted effort to listen to all I want to say, no matter how long or detailed it is.

When my husband shows me he appreciates even the little things that I do, it makes me happy and makes me want to do even more things for him. I find that I carry out my daily chores with more love and care when I feel appreciated.

When I am down, discouraged and just having a straight-out bad day, he will encourage me with the truth found in God's Word. He'll remind me that "our struggle is not against flesh and blood" (Eph. 6:12) and to "be strong in the Lord and in his mighty power" (Eph. 6:10).

My husband says "Thank you" to me almost daily for specific things I do, and that makes me feel appreciated. That, in turn, keeps me aware of what he is doing and what others are doing. I can put others first.

My husband is so willing to help me with the housework! Amen to that! We both work full-time at this point, and I just don't have the energy after working a full day to also tackle the housework, pay bills, shop for groceries and cook meals. My husband never gripes or complains when I ask him for help; in fact, he often sings or hums while he works, which cracks me up every time. In those moments, I feel especially close to him. Ninety-nine percent of the time my husband has the most amazing attitude toward the requests I ask of him. This has truly transformed my heart, because I had always struggled with my attitude in work and service-related things. My husband's positive attitude and constant support in our home have revealed Christ to me in a tangible way. I eagerly look for opportunities to serve my husband and bless him, and it is so easy for me because my husband has set the example by loving me as Christ loved the Church! That is the best thing a wife could ask for, in my opinion!

It was encouraging to discover how many men are really reaching out to build up and bring out the best in their wives. There are numerous ideas shared here that may help you respond in a new way to your wife. But remember that each woman is unique in her personality, needs, desires and spiritual gifts. Your task as a husband is to discover her uniqueness and respond accordingly. Just think of it as a project, and the discovery is giving you a road map on how to reach your destination.

TWO ADDITIONAL QUESTIONS

From a different survey, I discovered two other questions that women answered that deserve our consideration. The first question was:

What can a man do to make you feel good about yourself?

The answer that echoed from woman after woman related to their need for approval: "Women need approval. It's probably born in them—they need it in everything. That's why we take so much care to dress and put all this makeup on. We do it because we need approval—a compliment or acknowledgment that we're here and cared for by someone. That caring is one of the things I look for."

"Compliment me" was another answer I heard over and over again. Here are examples:

> Give small compliments in any area. The way I've fixed the house, my clothes, my makeup. Be alert to what I'm doing. Notice.

> Compliment me on how competent I am—like, "Gee, that was a really successful party we had" or "That was a nice trip, and I had a good time with you" or "That was a great piece of work you did."[1]

The second question that stood out as one of the easiest for the women to answer was:

> *If you had to give up hugging and caressing*
> *FOREVER, or sex FOREVER, which would you give up?*
> *The key word is "forever."*

Ninety-one percent of the women said they would give up sex with a man before they would give up his hugging and caressing. The women gave this question less thought than any other question. Their responses were instantaneous, almost to the point of being automatic. There seemed to be no doubt in their minds. If they had to choose, they would choose hugging and caressing over sex.[2] You may not like the answer, but perhaps it's a good subject to discuss with your wife.

AREAS THAT COULD STAND IMPROVEMENT

In our survey, we also asked wives what they wished their husbands would *not* do. You're probably thinking, *That was a dumb thing to do.* Yeah, perhaps. But once again the women came up with some helpful material for their men to consider.

One of the problems we have as men is being defensive. We don't like to hear suggestions or even constructive criticism. And we don't like to admit that we're wrong. Years ago, I read some information about men and their reaction to being wrong. It went like this: *Men hate to be wrong.* When I read that, I thought about it for a while and then said, "I don't agree with that."

The next points were:

1. Men hate to admit they might have been wrong.
2. Men hate it when their wives know they're wrong before they do.
3. Men think they're being made wrong by their wives when they're not!

That last point really convicted me, because I've thought that. And when a man thinks that, he tends to overreact.

Proverbs 28:13 has good advice for all of us: "A man who refuses to admit his mistakes can never be successful. But if he confesses and forsakes them, he gets another chance" (*TLB*). It's true. Admitting when you've made a mistake does wonders for your marriage. Here are some other biblical guidelines:

> If you refuse criticism you will end in poverty and disgrace; if you accept criticism you are on the road to fame (Prov. 13:18, *TLB*).

> Don't refuse to accept criticism; get all the help you can (Prov. 23:12, *TLB*).

> It is a badge of honor to accept valid criticism (Prov. 25:12, *TLB*).

How Do Your Answers Match Up with Reality?

The following responses are from wives who were asked the question, "What are some things you wish your husband wouldn't do?" As you read these responses, consider whether any of these comments describe you. The responses have been divided into six sections, with somewhat similar responses grouped together.

Group 1

Tell his friends when I get angry with him. Read the newspaper when I am trying to talk to him. Tease his sons when they are being sensitive. Complain that I'm too sensitive. Go through the day without a hug or kiss.

Sit in front of the computer and work and spend a lot of time on it.

Procrastinate. Dominate the conversation. Leave his plate at the table.

Point out things I do or don't do and then say that it is not really important. If it is not important, don't point out the flaw.

Leave his trash on the counter.

I wish my husband would not forget the things that we've talked about.

Silly things—sometimes I feel he doesn't always need to have the remote control; however, over the years he has learned to share the choice of viewing.

Make me worship like he does. I have my own style of worship that is not like my husband's.

Discount my attention to details.

Volunteer "us" to do things without asking me first in private.

Leave me to fend for myself when we are in a crowd or at an event.

Group 2

Get angry, so easily, over things that don't go his way or when we disagree about something. He tends to over-react and blow up over the smallest things. It makes him an unsafe person, and I can't relax and just be myself. I wonder when Mount Vesuvius will erupt next. It shuts down communication and damages intimacy and closeness.

Not be so judgmental of others. Clam up and not talk about something that is bothering him. I wish he would not avoid conflict and that he would learn to walk through the communication process of talking out problems right away rather than waiting until they build up and can't be ignored.

Go silent when something is wrong. That makes me fearful and nervous.

Not be critical. Try to fix when I don't want it fixed.

Sometimes he can "nag" about things and put pressure on me to be on "his schedule." Always thinks he's the one that's right.

Putting things off. Being moody or snappish toward me.

Gets angry so quickly, doesn't have any patience for questions or conversation regarding finances.

Watches TV or raises his voice.

Complains. If and when he complains about something it makes me feel like he's complaining about me, our life, the things we do. . . . He becomes distant and defensive and we end up arguing.

Interrupts me. I wish he wouldn't be so defensive. He is always looking for an easier way. Now, that can be good, but also not good. It's frustrating when I want something done as *I* want it done and then he ponders and goes for a different plan because to him it was simpler and easier. If I object, then I'm unappreciative and he's then angry.

Overly critical, impatient—overly reactive and loses his temper over little stuff. Trivializes what bothers me and what I'm upset about. I've been married 29 long years!

WHAT'S ALL THE SHOUTIN' ABOUT?

The three main responses and concerns in Group 2 are probably some of the most common of all. Read the section again. Do you see yourself in any of these comments?

Anger—that feeling of irritation that is often expressed more in tone of voice and nonverbal expressions can deaden the love of a wife for her husband. Because many men struggle with these feelings and lack a feelings vocabulary, anger is often used in response. Anger can be used to protect oneself from others and keep them from getting too close. Anger is actually a secondary emotion and is usually caused by fear, hurt or frustration. For help with the issue of anger, as well as conflict, you may want to read *Mad About Us—Moving from Anger to Intimacy with Your Spouse*, by Gary and Carrie Oliver.

It's true that we as men tend to avoid conflict if at all possible. Sometimes we feel overwhelmed by the process, especially if we've never learned a healthy pattern of resolving conflict. Avoiding conflict doesn't make it disappear; it only makes it grow larger. If you try to bury it, you only postpone a bigger problem. Conflict is a part of marriage, but it can be healthy and productive.

Group 3

I wish that he would not be sarcastic with me.

I wish he would not allow his irritations with me to come out in the form of snide remarks. Especially when it has to do with aspects of me that have caused us trouble and that I am working on.

Sometimes he gets into sarcastic "guy talk" mode where everything is a "dig" or a negative comment (because with his years in the military that is how they communicate). I wish he wouldn't talk that way to me. It's hard for him when coming out of that environment to home.

Reacting before knowing all the facts. Making comments under his breath.

Use of sarcasm; it is hurtful and exhausting to decipher what is a joke and what is really honest underneath the sarcasm. Speaking in absolutes—i.e., "You always . . ." "You never . . ."

Being critical or getting mad at me. Being sarcastic— even in fun. Being pessimistic.

Those are some serious concerns. Let's take a closer look at them.

IT'S NOT ALWAYS WHAT YOU SAY, IT'S HOW YOU SAY IT

Every couple will voice complaints from time to time. That's normal, and complaints can be voiced in a way that your wife will hear them and not become defensive. For example, instead of focusing on what annoys you, talk more about what you would appreciate her doing. Your wife is much more likely to hear you and consider your request. Talking about what you don't like only reinforces the possibility of its continuing with an even greater intensity.

The principle of pointing toward what you would like also conveys to her your belief that she is capable of doing what you have requested. Doing this consistently, along with giving praise and appreciation when your wife complies, will bring about a change.

Criticism is the initial negative response that opens the door for the other destructive responses to follow. Criticism is different from complaining in that it attacks the other person's personality and character, usually with blame. Most criticisms are overgeneralized ("You always . . .") and personally accusing (the word "you" is central). A great deal of criticism comes in the form of blame, with use of the word "should."

Criticism can be hidden under the camouflage of joking and humor. When confronted about it, the person who criticizes will avoid responsibility by saying, "Hey, I was just joking." It reminds me of the passage in Proverbs that says, "Like a madman who casts firebrands, arrows and death, so is the man who deceives his neighbor and then says, Was I not joking?" (Prov. 26:18-19, *AMP*).

Faultfinding is a common form of criticism. It's a favorite response of the perfectionistic spouse. Criticism is usually destructive, but it's interesting to hear critics say they're just trying to remold their partners into better persons by offering some "constructive" criticism. Too often criticism does not construct; it demolishes. It doesn't nourish a relationship; it poisons. And often the presentation is like this description: "There is one who speaks rashly like the thrusts of a sword" (Prov. 12:18, *NASB*).

Criticism that is destructive accuses and tries to make the other person feel guilty. It intimidates and is often an outgrowth of personal resentment.

BEWARE THE ZINGER

Criticism comes in many shapes and sizes. You've heard of "zingers," those lethal, verbal guided missiles. A zinger comes at you with a sharp point and a dull barb that catches the flesh as it goes in. The power of these sharp, caustic statements is seen when you realize that one zinger can undo 20 acts of kindness. That's right, 20.

A zinger has the power to render many positive acts meaningless. Once a zinger has landed, the effect is similar to a radioactive cloud that settles on an area of what used to be prime farmland. The land is so contaminated by the radioactivity that, even though seeds are scattered and plants are planted, they fail to take root. Subsequently, they die out or are washed away by the elements. It takes decades for the contamination to dissipate. The kind acts of loving words following the placement of a zinger find a similar hostile soil. It may take hours before there is a receptivity or positive response to your positive overtures.[3]

Another form of criticism is called *invalidation*. When invalidation is present in a marriage, it destroys the effect of *validation* as well as the friendship relationship of marriage. Encouragement is wiped out. Sometimes couples get along and maintain their relationship without sufficient validation, but they cannot handle continued invalidation. This is yet another example of one negative comment destroying 20 acts of kindness.[4]

Invalidation is like a slow, fatal disease that, once established in a relationship, spreads and destroys the positive feelings. As one wife said, "The so-called friend I married became my enemy with his unexpected attacks. I felt demeaned, put down, and my self-esteem slowly crumbled. I guess that's why our fights escalated so much. I had to fight to survive." To keep love and your marriage alive, keep the criticism out.

The next step down the path of destruction is contempt—the intent to insult or psychologically abuse your spouse. That sounds harsh, doesn't it? But that's what happens. It's like using a mortar in a battle to lob shells into the enemy lines. But in a marriage, you are lobbing insults into the person who you promised to love. It's thinking negative thoughts and speaking negative statements where nothing is sacred. Name-calling, nonverbal actions, sneering, put-downs and mocking are all part of the pattern.

It is all too easy to focus on the things we don't like about our mates, especially when we are irritated with them.

THE POWER OF POSITIVE REINFORCEMENT

The only effective solution is to balance any necessary criticism with at least five times as many compliments and expressions of gratitude. These don't have to be elaborate. In fact, it is better if they are a simple "Hey, thanks for taking care of that" or "I really appreciated such and such" or even "Your hair looks especially nice today." Similar comments let your mate know that you *are* paying attention. And because everybody loves approval, your spouse will tend to replicate the behavior you are rewarding her for with her gratitude. Professionally and personally, I have learned the power of catching someone being good.

Think of the wonderful fruit this intervention could bear in your relationship. In my own marriage, I know how well I respond when my wife acknowledges something I have done for her or compliments my appearance on a particular day. Besides making me feel good, I like pleasing her, and so I try to do those things more often. I don't think I am unique in this way. Everybody loves approval, but husbands and wives tend to be more stingy with it than they should. As a result, spouses end up feeling unappreciated by and isolated from each other.

Exceptional couples understand how their partner's strengths *and* weaknesses help them become better people. While no spouse wants his or her mate to have shortcomings, the fact is, we all do. Even if we are working to overcome them, from time to time our partner is going to stumble into our flaws, and vice versa. In such times, it is a very mature spouse who can see the opportunity for growth these situations present.

I will never forget one elderly gentleman—and he was a gentleman—who was taking exceptionally good care of his wife. Moreover, he seemed not to lose his patience like so many caregivers sometimes understandably do. I myself have a difficult time watching those I love suffer even from a head cold and, to my shame, I often allow such things to make me an insufferable crab—as if I had anything to complain about. But this man was so patient and loving in his ministrations to his wife that I finally asked him what his secret was.

"We've had a lot of good years together, and part of it is I figure I owe at least this much to her. But the other thing is that I've never been a very patient person. I used to complain a lot. It was mostly my way of blowing off steam. Anyway, seeing all that she's going through, and considering everything I've had to do, what with taking her to doctors and getting up at night to change her diapers and everything else, the little irritations in life don't seem to bother me so much anymore."

He started to tear up. "After all these years, she's still teaching me things."

I would invite you to look at yourself when your spouse's weaknesses and vulnerabilities are exposed and see what they can teach you about yourself.[5]

Group 4

I wish he wouldn't cuss and act differently when he is not around me—or be negative.

Group 5

I wish he wouldn't watch TV while I'm talking to him.

I wish he wouldn't try to fix a problem—just listen.

I really hate it when he dictates to me, like I'm an employee. I am a highly educated woman, yet he can make me feel so stupid. I really hate it when he treats our kids badly. This is an issue with us. He seems to favor one over the other, and it really creates tension for us.

Group 6

When I ask him to do something for me he waits or puts it off until later, and then I either get frustrated and do it myself, or it doesn't get done. Buying me gifts are things *he* likes/wants.

I would like him to move away from the exercise equipment aisle when it comes to buying me a gift and away from Costco as the only store to shop at.

He shuts down when I cry because he doesn't know what to do (a hug would make such a difference—if he would offer). He thinks it is best to get busy when sad—not cry. It bothers me when he does not make eye contact with me when communicating—makes it seem like he is disinterested and/or distracted.

Sometimes he thinks and plans too much—which I know is a good thing. Maybe he could do less of that and be more spontaneous. (Although he is a lot better as we get older.) Talk less about money—examples: worries a little. Can be dismissive of what I think is a problem and he doesn't.

He overeats. He goes overboard with things in his life.

He brings home stresses from work. Puts himself down. Belittles what a great dad and husband he is. His tone of voice sometimes when he talks.

Talks down to me. Tells me I'm emotional.

He defines my feelings and emotions for me. He says, "Don't build me the clock; just give me the time."

I wish he would give me clear communication and get to the point.

Sometimes he is too focused on what he has to get done—bills, whatever. I would love to see him let down, play golf, enjoy free time; of course, maybe if I would pay the bills, maybe he would have more free time. (I doubt it, I think he would find other things to get done.)

He works so many hours, makes too many commitments, and doesn't spend enough time at home.

I have a hard time even coming up with something. I guess if he could "reconstruct" the bathroom after using it in the morning, that would be great. Towels, toiletries and such scattered for me to put away each morning. Makes me feel disrespected or that he didn't care enough to put them away and expects me to do it. But I know that's not his intention—but it still feels that way. And clothes on the floor in various places in the house. Still roommate-y kind of stuff after all these years. But that's all!

I wish my husband would not be late for everything. When we go anywhere together, I am the one who gets the kids up, diapered, dressed, fed, packs the diaper bag, get myself dressed, fed, put shoes and coats on, gather necessities together—all while he reads the paper and takes a long shower . . . only to get in the car at the time we are supposed to be arriving at our destination. When I sit in the car with the kids waiting, that also means I have not had a chance to do my last-minute things, like use the restroom just before leaving. I often have car rides where I am stewing inside and say nothing about the three-ring circus I have just gone through . . . all to keep him happy.

He makes promises and does not follow through. He often gets sidetracked and forgets what he promised me. This hurts my heart. Also his being so prideful when he knows he has hurt my feelings; he would rather wait out my hurt and resentment than come to me and ask forgiveness or talk things out, for he knows I will "get over it." But what he really does not know is that until resolved, it is still there.

I wish my husband wouldn't lose his patience with me whenever I happen to be driving. I am already nervous when driving and become even more nervous when he is a backseat driver.

WHAT CHANGES WOULD YOU MAKE?

I discovered these women's concerns about their husbands by asking a different question: "If you could wave a magic wand and make one change in your man, what would you change?" Here are their responses:

Group 7
More self-control . . . reduce his temper.

That I could be number one in his life instead of number two to his work.

I would wand away his stubbornness.

I'd change his attitude about life, to take more time to smell the roses. Take time to remember anniversaries. Take a vacation. I think if he had taken more time with his family instead of chasing the dollar, we would still be married.

That it's all right to trust enough to fall head over heels in love with a woman.

I'd cut his domineering attitude.

I'd give him the ability to communicate better.

I'd have him not try so desperately to please his mother.

I would have him accept my independent spirit.

I would increase his self-confidence, which would cure many other problems.

I'd like for him to be more spontaneous.

I'd wave my magic wand and say, "Be more sensitive."

I'd like for him not to always criticize me.

I'd like him to be more of a partner with more involvement in decisions that affect our family.

I would have him forget my past.

I wish I could wave a magic wand and make my man feel inner strength enough to show his affection for me in public. In the store he walks far enough in front of me to make it appear we aren't together. When we eat out, he doesn't talk to me, but rather keeps looking over my head to see whoever else is there. That hurts. I want him to recognize me in public.

I want more hugging before sex, during and after. Especially after.

If I had a magic wand to wave, I'd make his working environment more pleasant. He loves his job but hates the workplace he's in.

I'd change his way of supposedly telling me he loves me. I'd prefer he showed me he loves me with true companionship. Actions speak louder than words.[6]

This last response is different but insightful. Perhaps this woman's journey and discovery will give you something to think about:

There are plenty of petty things that my husband does that annoy me, but those things are more my issues than his, because I am letting them annoy me in the first place. As for bigger issues, I wish my husband wouldn't pull away from affection so quickly. By affection, I mean things as simple as hugs and kisses. My husband is the king when it comes to serving me around our home, but his weakness is serving me with personal touch.

It has been a tremendous challenge for me to learn to be satisfied with so little physical affirmation, as that is one of my love languages, but it is most certainly not one of my husband's. I remember shortly after I got married that I was devastated because my husband had little need for intimacy at all. I wondered what was wrong with me, and I felt unattractive all the time because my husband didn't seem to desire me (not always, but more or less). I remember sitting at a Taco Bell (great food, too!) with my mom one day and my heart was so shattered at that point. I was sharing with her that I didn't know how to feel loved in a marriage that didn't provide the touch that I so longed for. I felt lonely; I felt ugly. My mom said something that I know was straight from heaven, because it pierced me to the core. She said, "Casey, if your husband didn't have arms, would you still expect him to hug you?"

I was annoyed initially, but I sat there thinking about what she said to me and I replied, "No, of course not." Then she told me, "Well, if God has not yet given your husband the emotional arms to hug you, is it healthy or fair of you to expect something that he cannot offer you at this time?" Those words sounded like jewels of wisdom pouring out of heaven for me. I was radically transformed after that conversation with my mom. I stopped expecting my husband to be something that he couldn't be, or at least wasn't at that point. I stopped hoping for things that would only disappoint me and bring bitterness between my husband and me.

Ultimately, I had to sacrifice my needs and lay them at the feet of Jesus—sweet surrender. Jesus sacrificed so much for me; His blood has washed away all of the horrible things that I have done in my life. The least that I can do with my life to honor that great sacrifice is to learn to do the same—less of me and more of Christ! I began to communicate to my husband when I needed a hug or a kiss, and though it isn't quite the same as getting affection spontaneously, it helped to satisfy my need for touch and it taught my husband new habits. My husband has always been willing to work on this area and that is what blesses me and keeps me pressing on in love. Communication was really the key to resolving that issue . . . and every other!

Discover the Encourager in You

1. Read the statements about what women hate on page 71. What are the five things your wife wishes you wouldn't do?

2. Read the statements from the wives in answer to the question, "What are some things you wish your husband wouldn't do?" (Group 1) on pages 72-73. What are the three major concerns the wives expressed?

3. If someone were to ask your wife right now how you encourage her, what would she say?

4. What type of comments, and perhaps a specific comment, stood out to you as something you would *not* hear from your wife? What words would you most deeply desire to hear from your wife?

5. You may be like the husbands whose wives described how they encourage and bless them. But if not, there are some attitudes and actions you need to ask God to remove; and there are some new attitudes and actions you need to ask God to cultivate in you. Spend a good amount of private time reflecting on all that you have read in this chapter, and then ask God what needs to change in you. When you have some answers, ask Him to change you. Then start thinking of ways you can do the following:

• New ways of thinking about my wife and her needs to change our home environment for the better
• Genuine praise of my wife—or of things she does—that I will begin speaking to her on a regular basis
• Sacrificial acts and ways of being that I will pursue to create a deeper friendship and intimacy with my wife

4

Understand
Your Wife

THE HUSBAND WHO TAKES THE TIME TO UNDERSTAND HIS WIFE is a wise man and is more likely to bring out the best in her. Not only that, but he will fulfill the teaching of Scripture: "You husbands . . . live with your wife in an understanding way" (1 Pet. 3:7, *NASB*). I can't get more bottom line than that. You are different from your wife and your wife is different from you. You need some basic understanding of those differences in order to live together in the way God intended. It's all pretty obvious; nevertheless, those differences can lead to misunderstandings. Here are some examples:

> Take bathrooms, for instance. A man has six items in his bathroom: a toothbrush, toothpaste, shaving cream, razor, a bar of Dial soap, and a towel from the Holiday Inn. The average number of items in the typical woman's bathroom: 437. A man would not be able to identify most of these items.

> What about the closet? A man has about four pairs of shoes: sneakers, sandals, casual and dress. If a woman

actually counts, she'll find she has 34 pairs of shoes, but she only wears about four of them.

And how about public restrooms? Men use restrooms for purely biological reasons. Women use rest rooms as social lounges. Men in a restroom would never speak a word to each other. Women who've never met will leave a restroom giggling together like old friends. And never in the history of the world has a man excused himself from a restaurant by saying, "Hey, Tom, I was just about to head to the restroom. Do you want to join me?"

When a woman says she'll be ready to go out in five more minutes, she's using the same measure of time a man uses when he says the football game's just got five more minutes left. Neither of them is counting time-outs, commercials or replays.[1]

Fact: Women don't think or express themselves in the same ways in which you do. Not only does her body work differently than yours, so does her mind. You're thinking, *I know that, so* . . .

You've probably already discovered that you don't think the same way she does. There's a big difference. You can have several choices of how you respond to this fact but only one of them will bring out the best in her. You could become irritated or exasperated with the differences or see that her differences complement yours and fill up some of your empty places.

Dr. Phil, the talk show host who has become a household name, struggled with these differences:

I am embarrassed to confess to you how many years I spent being frustrated with my wife, judging and resisting her for doing exactly what God designed her to do. God didn't design us to be the same; he designed us to be different. He made us different because we have different jobs in this world, and yet we criticize each other for being who we are.[2]

APPRECIATE THE DIFFERENCES

Your job is to identify the differences and learn to celebrate them. Differences can be an exchange of strengths. Each of you needs one another's differences. See them as an opportunity to be stretched rather than confined. It's true that some of the differences can prove to be irritants and sometimes inconvenient, but that's looking at just one side of them.

Here's a big step to consider. No husband can know what his wife is thinking even if he thinks he does. What's the point of saying this? Well, it simply means it may not be wise to take everything your wife says as reflecting what she's really thinking or feeling. In other words, don't take it for granted that you know what she is thinking or feeling just because that's what she says she's thinking or feeling. Does that make sense? If you've been married for a while, you've probably discovered this phenomenon even if it doesn't make sense. So, what's the action step?

Drop any assumptions you have about her and pray for an abundance of flexibility, because you're going to need it. Accept unpredictability in your wife. Think about this—what do you really know about your wife? To understand her, you need to know her thoughts and beliefs, even if they change.

How does she feel about:

- Being a mother?
- What she wants to be doing 10 years from now?
- Her childhood?
- Each of her siblings?
- What her losses in life have been?
- Her dad?
- Her mom?
- Your family?
- Your involvement with your family?
- What concerns her about raising the children?
- What concerns her about how you respond to the children?
- What concerns her about your work?
- Her career?
- Material items?[3]

For every one of these areas you don't know the answer to, it's essential that you find out. How do you learn? Watch your wife. Watch and observe and listen with the same intensity you give to a football game or video game. You'll see and hear things that have been evident for years.

One author suggests this approach, which could be applied to many other areas of your marriage:

You might start your observations the next time you visit a supermarket with your wife. During this mundane chore, you can learn something about the way her mind works if you step back and let her take the lead.

Let her decide which items to buy, which aisles to peruse, and how long to stay. You'll soon notice something about the way she thinks and makes decisions. Her methods of shopping are more than just consumer habits—they're clear signs of her personality. If she takes time to check prices, choose the bargain of the day, and use coupons, you'll learn that she's careful about how she spends money; this is a clue as to why she gets so angry when you pick up the tab when you go out to eat with your friends. (Money is at the top of the list of things couples argue about.)

What else can you notice? Does she plan out her trip so that she ends up in the frozen food aisle last so those foods are less likely to melt, or does she haphazardly choose her items? If she goes for the ice cream first, you'll have some insight into behavior that may drive you crazy at home when she doesn't plan ahead or think of the consequences of actions in the same way you do.

You can learn a lot if you just watch. Does she know exactly what she wants, or does she browse? Does she use a list or buy on impulse? Does she use her sense of sight or touch to buy produce? If you don't know the answers to these questions, there's a lot you don't know about your wife.[4]

It's difficult for your wife to feel special if you're not around her that much. One of the tasks we all have is discovering the balance between being at work and being with our wife. Sometimes our priorities are out of balance, when we place our wife toward the bottom of the list rather than near the top. I've seen too many men end up with a destroyed marriage because of an affair, and I'm not talking about another woman. They have an affair with their job, their hobby, the Internet, their friends or the like. An affair can occur whenever you take the time and energy that rightfully belongs to your wife and invest it elsewhere.

BE FULLY PRESENT

One of the other ways to make your wife feel special is to make sure you're home whenever you're home. That's right—be sure you're home when you're there. Most men catch on to this concept right away when I mention it. They may not say anything, but their nonverbals tell me they know exactly what I'm talking about. We all do it. It's called preoccupation. Our thoughts are elsewhere. It's possible for some husbands to be at home yet never really be at home. What do you do when you're at home, and what do you talk about? Think about that.

Here's one way to be sure you're fully present at home. Set aside a period of transition between work—or any potentially stressful activity—and other parts of the day. This transition time is designed to provide a "decompression period" so that any pressures, frustrations, fatigue, anger or anxiety that may have been generated will be less likely to affect marital communication. Some husbands pray as they drive home, committing the day's activities to the Lord. Others visualize how they are going to respond to each family member. One man said:

> "I live 20 miles from my bank. I've clocked off the halfway mark between my home and my bank by a telephone pole. I take the first ten miles up to that

point to think about my job. But when I arrive at that pole, I switch my thinking to my family. I prepare for our time together. I mentally get ready to greet them and spend time with them. When I leave for work the next morning, I spend my first ten miles reflecting on my family. When I pass my marker, I begin to prepare mentally for the day." Not surprisingly, that man was winning at home and the bank.[5]

Some couples take 20 minutes when they arrive home to sit in a dimly lighted room and listen to a recording of their favorite music, with very little talking.

When you, or your wife, are overly tired, emotionally upset, sick, injured or in pain, never discuss serious subjects or important matters that involve potential disagreement.

Set aside a special agreed-upon time every day to take up issues that involve making decisions, family business, disagreements and problems. This "Decision Time" should allow for the relaxed and uninterrupted discussion of all decision-making and problem-solving activities. No other activities should be involved, such as eating, driving or watching television. Take the phone off the hook. It may also help to set a time to talk.

Some couples have found it helpful to save all complaints about their marriage, disagreements and joint decisions for the scheduled Decision Time when these matters are taken up. Jot down items as they arise. When you pose a problem or lodge a complaint, be specific as to what you want from the other person. Do you want anger, defensiveness, resistance and continuation of the problem? Or do you want openness, cooperation and a change on the part of the other person? The way you approach the problem will determine your spouse's response.

THE MOST IMPORTANT THING YOU CAN DO

What does your wife need, or what does any wife need? She needs you to listen—to really listen. We men think we listen, but many of us don't understand how to do it.

One of the greatest gifts you can give to your spouse is the gift of listening. It can be an act of connection and caring. But far too many only hear themselves talking. Few listen. Often when two people are talking, they are, for the most part, dialogues of the deaf. They're talking *at* one another. If you listen to your wife, she feels, *I must be worth hearing.* If you ignore your wife, her thought could be, *What I said wasn't important* or *He doesn't care about me!*

Let me give you a threefold definition of listening when it pertains to your wife talking to you:

1. *Listening means that you're not thinking about what you're going to say when she stops talking.* You are not busy formulating your response. You're concentrating on what is being said and you're putting into practice Proverbs 18:13: "He who answers a matter before he hears the facts—it is folly and shame to him" (*AMP*); and James 1:19: "Understand [this], my beloved brethren. Let every man be quick to hear, [a ready listener], slow to speak, slow to take offense and to get angry" (*AMP*).

2. *Listening means that you're completely accepting of what is being said, without judging what she is saying or how she*

is saying it. If you don't like her tone of voice or the words used, and you react on the spot, you may miss the meaning. Perhaps she hasn't said it in the best way, but why not listen and then come back later—when both of you are calm—to discuss the proper wording and tone of voice? Acceptance doesn't mean that you agree with the content of what she says. It means that you acknowledge and understand that what she is saying is something that she's feeling.

3. *Listening means being able to repeat what she's said and express what you think she was feeling while speaking to you.* Real listening implies having an interest in her feelings and opinions and attempting to understand those feelings from her perspective.

If your wife shares a frustrating and difficult situation with you, you may stop listening because you view it as complaining. Or you may listen more closely because you view it as an act of trust in you.

GENDER DIFFERENCES AND LISTENING STYLES

Lack of understanding of gender differences in listening and conversation creates problems. Women use more verbal responses to *encourage* the talker. They're more likely than men to use listening signals like "mm-hmmm" and "yeah" just to indicate they're listening.

A husband will use this response only when he's *agreeing* with what his wife is saying. You can see what the outcome could be. A husband interprets his wife's listening responses as signs that she agrees with him. He's thinking, *All right! Good deal! We can get that new sports car!* Later on, he discovers she wasn't agreeing with him at all. He didn't realize she was simply indicating her interest in what he was saying and in keeping the interchange going. His wife, on the other hand, may feel ignored and disappointed, because he doesn't make the same listening responses she does. She interprets his quietness as not caring.

A man is more likely than a woman to make comments throughout the conversation. But a woman may feel bothered after she's been interrupted or hasn't been given any listening feedback. This is why many wives complain, "My husband always interrupts me" or "He never listens to me."

When it comes to your communication style, here's a recap of some things to keep in mind:

- Men are more likely to interrupt another person, whether the person is male or female.
- Men are less likely to respond to the comments of another person and, many times, make no response at all, or give a delayed response after the other finishes speaking. One shows a minimum degree of enthusiasm.
- Men are more likely to challenge or dispute statements made by their wives, which explains why men may seem to be argumentative.
- Men tend to make more statements of fact or opinion than women do.

What can a man do to be a better listener? Remember this, although it may be hard to accept: If your wife doesn't *feel* as though you're listening to her, it's the same as if you're not listening to her. If you're like me, your first response to this statement is to argue with it. "Hey, of course I'm listening. It's just her perception. Forget it."

Go back and read what I said again and again and again until it sinks in.

Here's what will cause your wife to say you're a good listener. When your wife is talking to you, stand still when she's talking. Just stop and stand still. It's hard to talk to a moving target, to a man in motion. You may think you can listen and move, and that may be true, but she won't believe it.

Next, stop—stop what you're doing. Put down the remote after you've turned off the TV. Don't answer that phone or respond to the text message. Give her 110 percent attention.

The next step is to look . . . at her. Turn your body so you are facing her, unless you're driving. And now listen—take it in—don't interrupt or try to fix. When you're talking, don't let your eyes wander. If you don't have eye contact, you miss out. Remember this fact: *Most women tend to repeat what they've said when they don't have eye contact with you because they're not sure if you have heard them.* Sound familiar? Husbands complain, "My wife always repeats; I heard her the first time!" Wives complain, "His eyes were all over the place. He can't do two things at one time. How do I know he heard me?"

The Eyes Have It

Listen with your eyes as well. Because of my retarded son, Matthew, who didn't have a vocabulary, I learned to listen to him with my eyes. I had no other option. He would grab our hands and place them on his head or rub his head against us to show us something was wrong. We learned to read his body movements and his eyes to detect any seizure activity. I could read his nonverbal signals that carried a message. Because of Matthew, I learned to listen to what my counselees could not put into words. I learned to listen to the message behind the message—the hurt, the ache, the frustration, the loss of hope, the fear of rejection, the joy, the delight, the promise of change. I reflect upon what I see on a counselee's face—his posture, walk, pace—and tell him what I see. This gives him an opportunity to explain further what he is thinking and feeling. He *knows* I'm tuned in to him.

Listen to others' tone of voice. Listen to your own. Listen to how with some speakers it's tone of voice that makes the difference. It's not loudness that makes a difference; it's tone.

How do you end your phone conversations? You don't come out and say you need to terminate the conversation, or that you're finished, do you? You use the change in tonal quality to accomplish this. One of my Shelties taught this to me years ago. Prince had this unique ability to figure out when I was concluding a phone conversation. He'd show up during the last 10 seconds of the conversation with a tennis ball in his mouth. It was as though he was saying, "I know you're about through. It's time to play ball." I thought, *What's this? A psychic dog?* No. He'd figure out the change in my voice and put two and two together. (I just hate it when the dog is smarter than me!)

I hate to admit it, but when it comes to tone of voice or variation of tone, men have more monotonous tones than women. Men don't open their jaws as wide as women, so they tend to sound more nasal than women. And men use only three vocal tones whereas women use more than five. So men tend to use more choppy staccato tones that can come across as abrupt and perhaps less approachable, at least to a woman. Women tend

to have more flowing tones. And a woman will tend to use vocal inflections to emphasize a point whereas a man uses loudness.[6] Sound familiar?

If your wife is one who gives the entire novel length story
at some other time than during the story, let her know you do
better and you can engage her better in conversation when it's
presented in smaller chunks.[7]

When Silence Isn't Golden

And above all, don't go silent on her. One of the most vicious
and destructive communication techniques is silence. It can
be devastating. Each person in a marriage needs to be recognized and acknowledged. But when we retreat into silence, our
wife feels her very presence, existence and significance is ignored by the most significant person in her life—you! In fact,
many consider silence an insult!

Silence can communicate a multitude of things: happiness, satisfaction, a sense of contentment, and wellbeing. But
more often than not it communicates dissatisfaction, contempt, anger, pouting, sulking, "who cares," "who gives a
darn," "I'll show you," and so on; when silence prevails there
is little opportunity to resolve issues and move forward in a
relationship. "Talk to me," she begs and we may get angry or
continue to withdraw through silence. Too many of us use silence as a weapon.

If you're feeling overwhelmed or at a loss for words (which
is not uncommon for us as men), share this with your wife.
Let her know that you're thinking or taking time to process
your response, but you *will* respond in a few minutes or before
a certain time. And we need to follow through and not hope
that she will forget it. That won't happen! We all know that.

John Gray, who is most recognized for his books on *Mars and Venus* (relationships between men and women), gives some helpful suggestions:

> To support your wife in feeling more loving and accepting, here is some bottom-line advice for men:
>
> 1. When you suspect she is upset, don't wait for her to initiate the conversation (when you initiate, it takes away 50 percent of her emotional charge).
>
> 2. As you let her talk, keep reminding yourself that it doesn't help to get upset with her for being upset.
>
> 3. Whenever you feel an urgent need to interrupt or correct, don't.
>
> 4. When you don't know what to say, say nothing. If you can't say something positive or respectful, keep quiet.
>
> 5. If she won't talk, ask more questions until she does.
>
> 6. Whatever you do, don't correct or judge her feelings.
>
> 7. Remain as calm and centered as possible, and keep a lock on your strong reactions. (If you lose control and "spill your guts" even for a moment, you lose and have to start all over at a disadvantage.)[8]

One of the best ways of responding and showing that you're listening is by reflecting back what you hear. Take a look at the following statements:

- "Kind of made (makes) you feel . . ."
- "The thing you feel most right now is sort of like . . ."
- "What I hear you saying is . . ."
- "So, as you see it . . ."
- "As I get it, you're saying . . ."
- "What I guess I'm hearing is . . ."
- "I'm not sure I'm with you, but . . ."
- "I somehow sense that maybe you feel . . ."
- "You feel . . ."
- "I really hear you saying that . . ."
- "I wonder if you're expressing a concern that . . ."
- "It sounds as if you're indicating you . . ."
- "I wonder if you're saying . . ."
- "You place a high value on . . ."
- "It seems to you . . ."
- "You appear to be feeling . . ."
- "It appears to you . . ."
- "As I hear it, you . . ."
- "So, from where you sit . . ."
- "Your feeling is now that . . ."
- "I read you as . . ."
- "Sometimes you . . ."
- "You must have felt . . ."
- "I sense that you're feeling . . ."
- "Your message seems to be, I . . ."
- "You appear . . ."
- "Listening to you, it seems as if . . ."
- "I gather that . . ."

None of these phrases are definite. None state what you believe or feel. None of them tells the other what to do or think or feel. They merely reflect what you think your wife is saying and give her the opportunity to say, "Yes, that's it," or "No, that's not what I was saying."

Remember that a major need your wife has of you is very basic: "Talk to me!" It can't be put in a simpler way. If you really want to bring out the best in your wife, create an atmosphere in which she has the freedom to be totally open and transparent with you and can reveal her deepest feelings. As she talks with you, she's presenting you with a road map on how to respond to her. Here are some guidelines that work in carrying on a conversation with your wife.

A CONVERSATIONAL ROAD MAP

A caring husband converses with his wife in a way that enables her to reveal her deepest feelings. Through conversation he learns how to meet many of her needs. But the conversation *itself* meets one of her most important marital needs: She simply wants him to talk to her.

Here is a list that summarizes the way you can impress your spouse with conversation. We've dealt with all of them; now it's time to put them into action.

1. Remember how it was when you were dating? You both still need to exhibit that same intense interest in each other and in what you have to say—especially about feelings.

2. A woman has a profound need to engage in conversation about her concerns and interests with someone who—in her perception—cares deeply about her and for her.

3. Men, if your job keeps you away from home overnight or for days on end, think about changing jobs. If you cannot, find ways to restore the intimacy of your marriage each time you return from an absence, so that your wife can begin to feel comfortable with you again. (If your wife does most of the traveling, the same principle applies.)

4. Get into the habit of spending 15 hours each week alone with your spouse, giving each other undivided attention. Spend much of that time in natural but essential conversation.

5. Remember, most women *fall* in love with men who have set aside time to exchange conversation and affection with them. They *stay* in love with men who continue to meet those needs.

6. Financial considerations should not interfere with time for conversation. If you don't have the time to be alone to talk, your priorities are not arranged correctly.

7. Never use conversation as a form of punishment (ridicule, name calling, swearing or sarcasm). Conversation should be constructive, not destructive.

8. Never use conversation to force your spouse to agree with your way of thinking. Respect your spouse's feelings and opinions, especially when yours are different.

9. Never use conversation to remind each other of past mistakes. Avoid dwelling on present mistakes as well.

10. Develop interest in each other's favorite topics of conversation.

11. Learn to balance your conversation. Avoid interrupting each other and try to give each other the same amount of time to talk.

12. Use your conversation to *inform, investigate* and *understand* each other.[9]

DISCOVER THE ENCOURAGER IN YOU

1. Which of the following statements best describe you and your wife when it comes to talking and sharing?

   a. We say a lot but reveal little of our real selves.
   b. We reveal our real selves but we don't say very much.
   c. We say a lot and reveal a lot of our real selves.
   d. We say little and reveal little of our real selves.

2. Which of the following statements best describe you when it comes to sharing with your wife about what you are really thinking, feeling, wanting or not wanting?

   a. I keep my inner self well hidden.
   b. I reveal as much as I feel safe to share.
   c. I let it all hang out.

3. Which of the following statements best describe you when it comes to your wife sharing with you what she is really thinking, feeling, wanting or not wanting?

    a. She seems to keep her inner self well hidden.
    b. She seems to reveal as much as she feels safe to share.
    c. She seems to let it all hang out.

4. Which of the following statements best describe some of the ways you avoid deep sharing when you and your wife are getting too close?

    a. I laugh or crack a joke.
    b. I shrug it off and act as if it doesn't matter.
    c. I act confused—like I don't know what is going on.
    d. I look angry so that she can't see into me too deeply.
    e. I get angry or huffy, especially when I am feeling vulnerable.
    f. I get overly talkative.
    g. I get analytical—hiding behind a wall of intellectualizing.
    h. I change the subject so I won't have to deal with it.
    i. I act strong, together, above it all—especially when feeling vulnerable.

5. Why do you think you avoid sharing in this way? What is the effect of avoiding sharing in this way with your wife? What would you be willing to do to build sharing into your relationship?[10]

Romancing **Your Wife**

LET'S TALK ABOUT ROMANCE—YES! Finally we get to the important stuff. But wait a minute; I said romance, not S-E-X. That's a part of romance, but sometimes we, as men, bypass the romantic part and move right on to sex. If so, we've left out what's really important to our wives. Women want to be romanced! Let's get to a bottom-line question: Would your wife describe you as romantic? Think about it for a minute. Would *you* describe yourself as romantic? If you answered yes to either question, why? Why would you be seen as romantic?

Perhaps we ought to take a closer look at romance so that you know what I'm talking about. So, what is it?

The word "romantic" has so many meanings, including:

- Has no basis in fact
- Imaginary
- Marked by the imagination or emotional appeal of the heroic, adventurous, remote, mysterious or idealized [each of these could be a paragraph in and of itself]
- An emphasis on subjective emotional qualities
- Passionate love[1]

Romance is made up of fantasy, emotion and non-rational delights. It's really something different from the ordinary. It's a special time or event for two individuals.

I consulted a national survey for the answer to what women in general say is the most important to them in a relationship. They said, "We need to feel appreciated, wanted and loved."[2] The bottom line is they want affirmation! Your wife needs to know that she's special to you. When this occurs, you're helping her to be her best.

Wives want to feel loved, appreciated and respected *for who they are*. Those are their own words. What can you do to make your wife feel that way? You can learn as much as you can about her. You may think that you already know everything about your wife, but most of us don't. For example, what would you say are five actions a husband could do that a wife would say are the most important to romance? (Remember, you're answering this from a woman's perspective.)

Based on a national survey, here is what several hundred women said. The survey listed a number of actions that men could take, and women were asked to rate actions from 1 to 5 according to their romantic value, with 5 being the most important to romance. Here are those that received the highest rating:

- He touches me with tenderness (4.7)
- He snuggles after making love (4.6)
- He treats me as the most special person in his life (4.6)
- He is available when I need help (4.6)
- He gives emotionally (4.5)
- He shares his thoughts and dreams with me (4.5)
- He arranges for us to have time alone (4.4, higher for women with children)
- He knows what makes me happy (4.4)
- He keeps in touch when we are apart (4.4)
- He is gentle in his lovemaking (4.4)

- He listens to me intently (4.4, higher for married women)
- He treats me special when I am sick or down (4.4)
- He gives me love notes, cards, poems for no special reason (4.3)
- He is playful when we are alone (4.3)
- He undresses me with loving care (4.3)
- He remembers our anniversary or special day (4.2)
- He tells me he loves me (4.2)
- He surprises me with small tokens of love (4.2, higher for women with children)
- He compliments me (4.2, higher for married women)
- He includes me in his plans (4.2)
- He arranges a romantic dinner in or out (4.1)
- He gives me flowers for no special occasion (4.1)
- He initiates spontaneous sex (4.0)[3]

Now that you've read the list, go back and use it to enrich your marriage and begin to bring out the best in your wife.

1. Look through the list and consider which actions you do at the present time.
2. Look through the list and consider how frequently you do these things.
3. Now think about which 10 of these would be the most important to your wife.
4. Finally, ask her—yes, ask her—which of these she would like you to do more often. You may think you already know, but let her decide. Sometimes what we do as husbands isn't enough, or it's so subtle that it doesn't connect. Believe me, clarifying this area can put a smile on both of your faces.[4]

NONSEXUAL TOUCH

Here's another major insight that wives reveal. This one may shock you. Wives constantly say they don't receive enough touch—gentle, nonsexual touch. I was married for 48 years to a wonderful woman, and then she died of brain cancer. When your partner dies, you tend to think of what you wish you'd done more of, and this is one of my regrets. I wish I had done it a hundred-fold, as it would have meant so much to Joyce.

What would your wife like to hear about when you talk? Wives have suggested that they want to hear about:

- How wonderful she looks
- How you miss her
- How good it is to be with her
- Plans for your future together
- What you like about your relationship (to meet her personal dreams, goals, and so on)
- Her interests (encourage her in them)
- How you met (reminisce about the wonderful beginnings)
- Why she's special to you
- Positive things about the restaurant (or in whatever place you and she are together)
- Her accomplishments
- Her day
- Her ideas
- The appreciation you have for all she does[5]

If you respond with these items, she knows she's a priority. She knows she's in your thoughts. This works.

Romance was a major part of my relationship with Joyce—before and during marriage. We tried to be creative and not predictable. For example, we created a romantic atmosphere in our family room at home. For our twenty-fifth wedding anniversary, instead of spending money on a trip, we had our backyard landscaped to resemble a miniature mountain scene. We had a little (four-foot) hill, a waterfall and a trickling stream that feeds a couple of pools. There was a small footbridge and pine, birch and liquid amber trees, which provided us with ample fall colors. Our mountain scene could be viewed from our family room through sliding glass doors.

Some evenings, Joyce and I would play one of our favorite John Denver albums (that dates us) on the stereo, turn out the lights and sit together on the couch holding hands, listening to the music of the record and the waterfall. The outdoor lights accented the waterfall and the trees. We may have sat there for 30 or 40 minutes, not saying much, but listening and enjoying and feeling very content and comfortable. It was a romantic time for us. There were other times of romance, too, but I'm not going into detail on those!

WHAT MAKES ROMANCE?

A romantic relationship can have a number of important ingredients. First, romance often includes the element of the unexpected. The routines and tasks of our daily lives consume most of our time and energy. An unexpected romantic surprise can help break up the routine and monotony of the day. Surprises also carry the message, "I'm thinking about you. You're on my mind. I want your day to be different."

Romance Is Surprising

Presenting flowers for no special occasion or no special reason adds to the sense of romance. I enjoyed creating surprises for

Joyce. They ranged from the humorous to the serious. Because we enjoyed eating out together, I would often search out a new restaurant that I thought she would enjoy and take her there without telling her where we were going. I even took her on brief trips that were a total surprise to her. Sometimes she opened a cupboard to find a banner I'd placed there that said, "I love you."

You may have your own routine established for creating special romantic surprises. That's important. But beware: Anything that is repeated month after month, year after year or decade after decade may become humdrum. Surprising your spouse with dinner out at the same restaurant every payday may not be as romantic after 20 years! Why not look for new restaurants, activities and ways to say "I love you" that keep the excitement of the unexpected in your romancing?

Romance Is a Time for Two

A second element in a romantic relationship is called dating—something you used to do and hopefully still do. Dating means selecting a specific time to be together and making plans for the event. Sometimes a couple mutually plan the activity, or one person may be appointed to plan the date.

Most of the time, romantic dating is just for the two of you and not a crowd!

We asked wives what they *don't* want to talk about on a date. Now, you may wonder if these suggestions are necessary. Based on what women have said, they are, and they will not only save you some grief but also will build up your wife and your relationship.

Just imagine that you're at a quiet, quality restaurant, and that you have two hours to eat and connect. What will you talk about? Let's consider what your wife *doesn't* want to hear. On a date, wives don't want to hear about:

- Children or in-laws
- Your work
- Your involvement in something that doesn't involve her
- Anything negative—what you don't like
- Ongoing disagreements
- Tasks at home
- Money issues
- What's wrong at this restaurant
- What you've accomplished

Talk about yourselves. Make it a fun time. Laugh and enjoy each other and be a little crazy. When you go to a restaurant, let the host or hostess know that you and your spouse are there on a date.

Dates ought to center on an activity where you can interact together. If you attend a movie or play, plan time before or after the show to eat and talk together.

I've been impressed with some ministers who have made an announcement like the following from the pulpit: "If any of you ask my wife and me to attend a gathering on the first or third Friday of the month, we will thank you for the invitation, but we will have to decline. Those nights are our date nights together and we do not let anything interfere with those special evenings. And if any of you would like to know what we do on a date, you're free to ask!" An announcement like that may send some shock waves through the congregation. Couples in leadership, however, who make romance a priority, provide healthy role models for all the couples in the congregation.

Romance Isn't Always Practical

Third, because romance is often emotional and non-rational, a romantic relationship sometimes includes the impractical. You may splurge on an outing or a gift, which you know you can't really afford, but the romantic value makes it worth scrimping in other areas to pay for it. Or consider an out-of-the-ordinary event like inviting your spouse to a "famous" French restaurant in the countryside. Pack an inexpensive picnic dinner and take a tape recorder with some French songs and a picture book on France from the library to look through together.

Impractical romantic happenings are moments to remember. And that's what romance is so often built upon—good memories. Store your hearts with romantic memories and they'll carry you through the difficult times.

Romance Gets Out of the Rut

A fourth element in a romantic relationship is creativity. The French picnic dinner is an example of creative romance. Discover what delights your wife and make those delights happen in many different, creative ways. Even the way you express your love to your wife each day can be varied and innovative. If your wife can predict what you will say, how you will respond, what kind of gift you will give on special occasions, then you're in a romantic rut.

I like what Joseph Dillow tells husbands about being creative lovers. He has developed the following lighthearted test to help husbands evaluate their creativity in romance. Give yourself 10 points for each item on the following list if you have done it once in the past six months. If you have done any item on the list two or more times, give yourself 20 points.

Lover's Quotient Test

- Have you phoned her during the week and asked her out for one evening that weekend without telling her where you are taking her? Mystery date.

- Have you given her an evening completely off? You clean up the kitchen; you put the kids to bed.

- Have you gone parking with her at some safe and secluded spot and kissed and talked for an evening?

- Have you drawn a bath for her after dinner? Put a scented candle in the bathroom, add bath oil to the water, send her there right after dinner and then you clean up and put the kids to bed while she relaxes. (My wife says in order to get any points for this you must also clean up the tub!)

- Have you phoned her from work to tell her you were thinking nice thoughts about her? (You get *no* points for this one if you asked what was in the mail.)

- Have you written her a love letter and sent it special delivery? (First class mail will do—emails and texting don't have the same impact.)

- Have you made a tape recording of all the reasons you love her? Give it to her wrapped in a sheer negligee!

- Have you given her the day off? You clean the house, fix the meals and take care of the kids. (My wife says you ought to get 30 points for this!)

- Have you put a special effects stereo recording of ocean waves on tape and played it while you had a nude luau on the living room floor? (If this seems a little far out for your tastes, you could substitute by either removing the stereo effects or having a pop-corn party in the privacy of the bedroom instead.)

- Have you spent a whole evening (more than two hours) sharing mutual goals and planning family objectives with her and the children?

- Have you ever planned a surprise weekend? You make the reservations and arrange for someone to keep the children for two days. Tell her to pack her suitcase, but don't tell her where you are going. (Just be sure it's *not* the Super Bowl!) Make it someplace romantic.

- Have you ever picked up your clothes just one time in the past six months and put them on hangers?

- Have you given her an all-over body massage with scented lotion and a vibrator?

- Have you spent a session of making love to her that included at least two hours of romantic conversation, shared dreams, many positions of intercourse and much variety of approach and caresses?

- Have you repaired something around the house that she has *not* requested?

- Have you kissed her passionately for at least 30 seconds one morning just before you left for work, or one evening after you walked in the door?

- Have you brought her an unexpected little gift like perfume, a ring or an item of clothing?

- Have you replaced her old negligee?

I have given this ridiculous test to men all over the country. Let's see how your score compares with theirs:

200–360: Lover. You undoubtedly have one of the most satisfied wives in all the country.

150–200: Good. Very few make this category.

100–150: Average. This husband is somewhat typical and usually not very exciting as a lover.

50–100: Klutz. Too many men score in this category. I hope you'll begin to move up soon.

0–50: Husband. There is a difference between a "husband" and a "lover." The only reason your wife is still married to you is that she's a Christian, she has unusual capacity for unconditional acceptance and there are some verses in the Bible against divorce.[6]

While the test shouldn't be taken too seriously, it does outline a plan of attack to increase your creativity level. I realize

Romancing Your Wife

that many things on the list may not fit your temperament and your marriage relationship. *Make up your own list.* The idea is simply to encourage creativity in a fun way.

Romance Begins in the Mind

Fifth, romance involves daily acts of care, concern, love, speaking your partner's love language, listening and giving each other your personal attention. Such acts convey a message of acceptance and thoughtfulness to your spouse. You see, romance begins in your mind and not in your sex gland. Too many people, especially men, tend to let their physical drive take the lead in romance all the time. Rather, a thoughtful, caring attitude will create romance even when your glands are stuck in neutral.

Romance Is Defined by Commitment

Sixth, romance involves commitment. Every day of your life as a couple is marked by highs and lows, joys and disappointments.

Let's go back to affection. Affection and romance go hand in hand.

Affection—when you read this word, what comes to mind? For many men, it's sex. Let's eliminate this word "sex" from our vocabulary for a while. Now describe what affection means to you. Does it have the same meaning to your wife? Are you sure? The reason I'm pushing on this question is this: For a wife, affection is actually the "cement of your relationship." To most women, affection symbolizes security, protection, comfort and approval. When you show your wife affection, you're sending her several messages:

"I'll take care of you and protect you. You are important to me, and I don't want anything to happen to you."

"I'm concerned about the problems you face, and I am with you."[7]

Hugging, touch, cards, flowers, invitations can all be expressions of affection, but they frequently and consistently need to be a part of the equation, rather than once in a while. This is both reasonable and attainable. By answering the following questions, you'll have a better understanding of this part of your relationship.

1. On a scale of 1 to 10, with 10 being "very affectionate," how affectionate am I toward my wife? How would she rate me?
2. Is affection the environment for our entire marriage?
3. In the past, have I tended to equate affection with getting sexually aroused? Why hasn't this worked?
4. In what specific ways do I show my wife affection?
5. Would I be willing to have her coach me in how to show her more affection in the ways she really likes it?[8]

Being consistently affectionate—and not just at those times when one is interested in sex—is a highly valued positive response. Sometimes nothing is shared verbally. It can be as simple as sitting side by side and touching gently or moving close enough that you barely touch while you watch the sun dipping over a mountain with reddish clouds capturing your attention. It could be reaching out and holding hands in public. It can be something thoughtful, unrequested and noticed only by your partner.

When your wife has had a rough day, you may choose just to stroke her head or rub her shoulders instead of talking about what happened. Being so understood by you and meeting her needs gives her the assurance that she has indeed married the right person.

Nonsexual touching as well as sexual is important. Hugging is an important element of touching. And hugging is a vital expression of love. I know. I went for 15 years without receiving a hug from our son Matthew. It wasn't that he held back or didn't care. He wasn't capable. Matthew was a profoundly mentally retarded boy who died at the age of 22 and had the mental ability of about an 18-month-old. He lived in our home until he was 11 and then moved to Salem Christian Home in Ontario, California.

For years, Joyce and I affectionately reached out to Matthew with hugs and kisses, but he did not respond. Through this process we learned to give love without receiving love in return. And we accepted Matthew's limitation even though we eagerly looked forward to the time when we might receive a hug from him.

Then one day we wrapped our arms around Matthew and, for the first time, felt his arms reaching around us and squeezing. It is hard to describe how precious Matthew's hug was to us after living without it for so many years. After that first hug there were several other times when Matthew would respond with his simple embrace. And sometimes we held out our arms and said, "Matthew, hug," and he reached to give us a hug. Please—never take the expression of a hug for granted.

How would you respond to a doctor who prescribed that you receive four hugs a day? Physical hugging is very therapeutic. Hugging can lift depression and breathe new life into a tired body. When you are physically touched, the amount of hemo-globin in your body increases significantly. The surge of hemo-globin tones up the whole body, helps prevent disease and speeds recovery from illness.[9]

Do you hug your spouse? Do you receive hugs? One of my favorite quotes is, "Every marriage needs to be picked up and hugged and given personal attention."[10] Hugging is a signifi-cant way to bring out the best in your wife.

Affection is demonstrated in many ways and displays. Years ago, I heard the story of a couple who had been invited to a potluck dinner. The wife was not known for her cooking abil-ity, but she decided to make a custard pie. As they drove to the dinner, they knew they were in trouble, for they smelled the scorched crust. Then, when they turned a corner, the contents of the pie shifted dramatically from one side of the pie shell to the other. The husband could see his wife's anxiety rising by the moment.

When they arrived, they placed the pie on the dessert table. The guests were serving themselves salad and then went back for the main course. Just before they could move on to the desserts, the husband marched up to the table, looked over the number of homemade desserts and snatched up his wife's pie. As others looked at him, he announced, "There are so many desserts here, but my wife so rarely makes my favorite dessert that I'm claiming this for myself. I ate lightly on all the other courses, so now I can be a glutton."

And a glutton he was. Later his wife said, "He sat by the door eating what he could, mushing up the rest so no one else would bug him for a piece, and slipping chunks to the hosts' Rottweiler when no one was looking. He saw me looking at him and gave me a big wink. What he did made my evening. My husband, who doesn't always say much, communicated more love with what he did than with any words he could ever say."

ACTS OF CARING

Of course, there are many other ways to take positive action to show that you care. I raise flowers all year long, and I knew Joyce enjoyed seeing them inside the house. Often, after I made the morning coffee, I would cut her a rose and put it in a vase by her cup. It almost became automatic, but the motivation was the same. And often when I traveled, Joyce slipped a love note into my pants pocket.

Perhaps you're in the store and you see a favorite food your spouse enjoys, and you buy it for him or her even if you hate it; or you decide to stop at the store for an item, and you call your spouse at home or at work to see if there's anything he or she wants or needs. You are "other" thinking rather than "self" thinking. You follow through with the scriptural teaching in Ephesians 4:32: "Be kind and compassionate to one another."

An act of caring can be a phone call to ask if your wife has a prayer request. Acts of caring can mean remembering special dates and anniversaries without being reminded. I am amazed at the number of wives who have been deeply hurt by their husband over the years because he did not remember anniversaries or even birthdays.

And the men's excuses are so lame. I've heard, "I just didn't remember" and "I need to be reminded" and "We just didn't do that in our family." That's all such responses are—excuses! If the husband is sitting in my counseling office, I simply ask him if he forgets to go to work or to get involved in his hobby. Reluctantly, he says no, and I go on to let him know that I believe he is capable of learning something new that will benefit both his life and his wife's. We then talk about how he will do it. We don't accept excuses when it is obvious that change can occur.

SHOWING APPRECIATION AND EMPATHY

Another positive is being appreciative. This means going out of your way to notice all the little positive things your wife does and letting her know you appreciate her. It also means focusing on the positive experiences and dwelling upon those rather than the negative (more will be said about this later). Working toward agreement and appreciating the other's perspective is important. Compliments convey appreciation, but they need to be balanced between what a person does and who she is. Affirmations based on personal qualities are rare but highly appreciated.

Showing genuine concern for your wife when you notice she is upset builds unity and intimacy in your relationship. You may not be able to do anything, but sharing your desire to do so may be all that is necessary. When your wife shares a problem with you, don't relate a similar problem you once had, tell her what to do, crack jokes to cheer her up, or ask how she got into that problem in the first place. Instead, listen, put your arm around her, show that you understand, and let her know it's all right for her to feel and act the way she does.

I'm sure you've heard the word "empathy" time and time again. This is the feeling of being with another person both emotionally and intellectually. It's viewing life through your wife's eyes, feeling as she feels and hearing her story through her perceptions.

In marriage you have a choice to respond with empathy, sympathy or apathy. Sympathy is being overly involved in the emotions of your wife. It can actually undermine your emotional strength. Apathy means you couldn't care less. There are no in-betweens.

Empathy, however, includes rapport—knowing how your wife would feel in most situations without her having to explain. You'll experience something together at the same time through the eyes of your wife.

THE LIGHTER SIDE

Having a sense of humor and being able to laugh, joke and have fun gives balance to the serious side of marriage. Some of what you laugh at will be private, and some will be shared with others. Sometimes the memories are some of those hilarious incidents that happen even though your partner didn't think it was so funny at the time.

Several years ago, while speaking at a family camp at Forest Home, California, such an event happened to Joyce and me. We were staying in a nice cabin, and since I'm an early riser, I went down to the dining hall for an early breakfast, knowing that I would bring her back some fruit and a muffin. I entered the cabin and was just about ready to go into the bedroom with her food when the door of the bathroom was flung open. Joyce, fresh out of the shower, said, "Don't go in there! It's still there! Don't take my food in there!"

I was shocked and said, "What? What's in there?"

"In there!" she said again, almost in tears by now. "It's still in the bedroom. It was terrible. And don't you dare laugh. It wasn't funny!" I still didn't know what she was talking about, but saying to a husband, "Don't you dare laugh!" is like a subtle invitation that may get played out later.

Finally, she calmed down and told me what happened. She had been in bed, drinking her coffee, when she decided to reach down and pick up her slippers. She found one, lifted it up and then thrust her hand under the bed to find the other one. Now, Forest Home was using new mousetraps that consisted of a six-by-six-inch piece of cardboard with an extremely sticky substance on it. When a mouse stuck in it, it was stuck permanently and would eventually die. Well, you can guess what happened. Not only did Joyce put her hand directly on the goo substance, but it also contained a bloated dead mouse! It was gross! (I have a picture of it.) As she said, she went ballistic with screams, trying to dislodge this disgusting creature from her hand.

As Joyce was telling me all this, she was shaking her hand and demonstrating how she had tried to dislodge the mouse from her hand. The more she did this the funnier it got. I was biting the inside of my mouth to keep from smiling while remembering those fateful words, "Don't you dare laugh. It's not funny." I think she saw my struggle, because with an exaggerated put-out look, she said again, slowly, "*It's not funny.*"

That's all it took. I was a dead man, and I knew it. I laughed until the tears rolled down my face. I did take the mouse out and get rid of it. I also told Joyce that I would have gone into hysterics as well if that had happened to me, and that she had every right to be upset. After several hugs, she said, "I guess it was pretty funny at that." This became one of our favorite stories.

We also have many funny memories in which I was the source of the amusement. Joyce had a whole list of them.

Positive marriage shares the sense of shared joy. You share your wife's excitement and delight and you want her to be aware of what you're experiencing as well. Joy is a sense of glad-

Romancing Your Wife

ness, not necessarily happiness. It's also a command from Scripture: We are to "rejoice with those who rejoice" (Rom. 12:15).

ACCEPT ONE ANOTHER

Accepting each other for who you are and what you say is the goal. Acceptance means letting your wife know that even though you don't agree with what she is saying, you are willing to hear her out. It means freeing your wife from being molded into the fantasy you want her to be. It's more than tolerance. It's saying, "You and I are different in many ways. It's all right for you to be you and for me to be me. We are stronger together than we are separately, as we learn to complement one another." This doesn't mean spouses won't help to change each other—that's inevitable. But the purpose for which it's done, and the method, makes a world of difference.

DISCOVER THE ENCOURAGER IN YOU

1. Romance—are you good at it or not? The bottom line is that some men are and some men aren't. Let's discuss what you know with a couple of questions (you can ask your wife to discover if you answered correctly or not):

   • Romance to a woman means:

   _____

   _____

   • Romance to my wife means:

   _____

   _____

2. What is romantic about you and your wife's daily life together? What actions on your part create romance for you? What actions on your spouse's part create romance for you?

3. Describe a romantic getaway you would like to experience with your spouse. Where would it be? What would you do? How would it be different from your daily life? What would you wear? Where would you eat? What would be the décor, music, fragrances, conversation topics, and so on?

4. What would it take for this to actually happen? How could you create at home what you just described?

5. When you and your wife were dating, how did you create and sustain romance?

6. Which of the following statements best describe your current estimation on the degree of romance in your marriage?

   a. Our life together is one sustained romantic "high."
   b. We are romantic, but at times I feel we are getting less and less so.
   c. We have a romantic side of us that we can turn on when we want to.
   d. Maybe someday we will be able to be romantic.
   e. We're too old for romance.
   f. Romance? Who needs it? We are sensible and stable.
   g. We have more important things to do than get involved with romance.
   h. What's romance?

6. Which of the following statements best describe your relationship when it comes to romance?

    a. I am the romantic; my wife is practical and realistic.
    b. My wife is the romantic; I am practical and realistic.
    c. Both of us are romantic, but in our own way.
    d. Neither of us has a romantic bone in our body.

7. How do you feel when you get romantic and your wife doesn't respond? How do you feel when she gets romantic and you don't respond?

8. Which of the following statements best describe some of the reasons you are unable to get romantic with your wife?

    a. I am too critical of her.
    b. I feel she is critical of me.
    c. I hold too many resentments from the past.
    d. My mind is elsewhere, like on daily practical concerns.
    e. I'm concerned that she might reject me or not respond when I become romantic.
    f. I like to get romantic first because I am more of an initiator than a responder.

9. What is one way you would like you and your wife to be romantic at this point in your marriage?[11]

God's Plan
for Husbands

THIS IS A CHAPTER MOST MEN WILL LIKE. IT'S BRIEF, BLUNT AND TO THE POINT.

Whether you like the content or not . . . well, that remains to be seen. It's not meant to lay a burden on you, elicit guilt or point a finger at you. It's meant to help in your understanding of marriage and clarify your calling as a husband. It's meant to help you in your journey of being a positive support to your wife.

Let's begin with a question. You may need to stretch your memory a bit.

Why did you marry your wife? Your answer might include one or more of the following statements spoken by other men:

- "I wanted to share my life with someone."
- "I wanted someone to help make me happy."
- "I wanted to spend my life with someone I love and with someone who loves me."
- "I wanted to be happy and I wanted her to be happy."
- "I didn't want to spend my life alone."
- "I wanted to make up for all that was lacking in my own home."

- "I wanted to be faithful to God and love someone He wanted me to love."
- "I didn't want to end up alone, especially when I get older. Marriage is a security."

Did any of those answers resonate with you? Although personal happiness is part of the marriage equation, if that's all you think of as the reason you married, you need to go down a bit deeper. Let's take a look at what marriage is and discover its purpose.

Marriage is . . . a gift.

Marriage is . . . an opportunity for love to be learned.

Marriage is . . . a journey in which we as the travelers are faced with many choices and are responsible for these choices.

Marriage is . . . affected more by our inner communication than our outer communication.

Marriage is . . . often influenced by unresolved issues from our past than we realize.

Marriage is . . . a call to servanthood.

Marriage is . . . a call to friendship.

Marriage is . . . a call to suffering.

Marriage is . . . a refining process. It is an opportunity to be refined by God into the person He wants us to be.

Marriage is . . . an opportunity to reflect God's image.

When we marry for personal happiness and satisfaction, and then, for whatever reason, these start to diminish or have never met our standards, we tend to begin entertaining all sorts of unconstructive thoughts. I've heard people complain, "Why didn't He make men and women different than He did? It would make marriage so much easier." But why should God make it easier? Did He create marriage to make us happy or to make us holy?[1]

I talked with a couple in their late twenties who had been married for five years. In the third year, they had considered divorce. This is what they told me:

> We entered into marriage with high hopes and great expectations. Finally, we'd found someone that would make us happy. I had this dream but it ended up being more like a vapor. She didn't measure up, and neither did I. We always wanted more. We wanted the other to be better. We began to criticize and demand: "You're not meeting my needs. You're not the person I thought I was marrying." And then one of us mentioned the *D* word. We looked at one another and said, "No, never. There's got to be a better way."
>
> So we began to ask, *What does God want for our marriage?* After a hard two years, we've discovered a new way of living. Each morning, we ask, "What *will* please God in our marriage today?" The more we do this, the more satisfied we are with one another. The other way didn't work. This does. I'm just sorry we didn't start out that way.

GOD'S PURPOSE FOR MARRIAGE

The purpose of marriage is to please God. We need to remind ourselves of this each day, then take note of our words and actions and ask, *Does this please Him?* This is a safeguard. It provides a hedge of protection around a marriage.

We all need to discover God's design, not our own, for marriage. Marriage matters to God. He had a purpose in mind when He created marriage. God had two relational goals in mind. First, He created a person in His image so that He and the image-bearer could be in fellowship together. Then, seeing the aloneness of this first image-bearer, God made another like the first *and* like God, so they could *both* be in fellowship with each other *and* with Him.

God's Image-Bearer

God has a plan—and it happens in marriage—for transforming each of us into *image-bearers*. The bottom line is that that's what you are. What would happen if you looked in the mirror each morning and said, "I am an image-bearer"? We are called to reflect the glory of God in the marriage relationship. Unfortunately, this is not what most couples have in mind as their purpose when they enter into marriage. They have another purpose.

But God's main purpose is *not our* happiness.

Your marriage is not only going to change you, but it will also transform you. Have you heard the term "whistle-blower"? Depending on who's doing the talking, the phrase may be expressed with appreciation or scorn. It's a term used to describe someone who has revealed or exposed the truth about a person or a situation. A whistle-blower brings to light what was previously hidden. That's what marriage is, a whistle-blower. Marriage exposes and reveals who you really are when you enter into that covenant relationship. All the hidden places—and yes, defects too—will be made obvious. You'll be "found out." But that's all right! It's a great place for the process of transformation to occur!

A Transformed Heart

Transformation. It's an interesting word. Transformation is the heart of marriage. Yet many Christian couples have never integrated a pattern of Christian growth into their marriage. This is unfortunate because the two are so closely intertwined. They really can't run alongside one another on parallel tracks.

Scripture says that we are to be conformed to the image of Christ (see Rom. 8:29) and that Christ is to be formed in us (see Gal. 4:19). The results of this process should be evident in the marriage relationship. They're part of the script.

Both of you—you and your spouse—are quite different but equal in the eyes of God. In the New Testament, Paul reiterates this when he says that in Christ there is neither male nor female (see Gal. 3:28). This impacts the way you are to treat one another. We're called to *glorify* one another, not degrade.

If we were to see our spouse as someone to be used or abused, we're not responding to our spouse to the glory of God. We can insult the image of God in other ways as well. A friend of mine described it in very practical terms: "When you take someone for granted, you demean him or her. You send the unspoken message, *You are not worth much to me.* You also rob this person of the gift of human appreciation. And to be loved and appreciated gives all of us a reason to live each day."

When the gift is withdrawn or denied over the years, a person's spirit begins to wither and die. A couple may endure this hardship and stay married for decades, but they are only serving a sentence. In long-term marriages where one spouse or both are continually taken for granted and not built up, a wall of indifference arises between that husband and wife.

So the first question to ask yourself is, *What is it like being married to me?* Take some time to reflect on this question. Take a day, or better yet, take a week and carry a 3x5-inch index card around with you. When a thought comes to mind, write it down. When you ask yourself a question, it's like looking into the mirror. You'll see areas where you can say, "I'm doing all right there." But you'll discover other areas where you'll say, "I need some work."[2]

Now the hard question. Ask your *wife* to answer this question for you: "What is it like being married to me?" Have her take several days to process the question before answering. If you really want some help, you could ask, "In what area or areas would you like to see some improvement?" If you ask this, assure her that no matter what she suggests, all you will say is, "Thank you for letting me know this."

Every movie and every play has a script to follow as well as a writer, producer and director. Well, we have a script for our lives and our marriage. Where there are many different writers, producers and directors in the movie world, there is only one Writer, Producer and Director in your life and in your marriage—and that Person is God.

How to Lead in Your Marriage

According to His script, a husband has several callings, one of which is to be a leader, or "the head of the wife." Let's concentrate on this one. What does that mean? It doesn't mean control, passive noninvolvement, asserted superiority or taking advantage. On the contrary, a husband must never use his role as leader for selfish benefit. To do so would deviate from God's plan.

A husband must never put his wife into a straitjacket of compliance, or she will wither and so will her love for him. Even recent secular research has shown that what kills the love of a spouse for the other is in direct violation of Scripture—i.e., attempting to control rather than serve your partner. In the book *The Power of a Praying Husband,* there's great insight.

The power of a praying husband is not a means of gaining control over your wife. We all know that never really happens anyway. That's because God doesn't want us controlling other people. He wants us to let *Him* control *us*. When we humble ourselves before God and let *Him* control *us*, then He can work through us. God wants to work through you as an instrument of *His* power as you intercede in prayer for your wife. The power in your prayer is God's.[3]

A husband is to lead sacrificially in his marriage by example, not by ordering or constantly instructing his wife. He is never, and I mean *never*, to tell his wife what the Scriptures say *she* is to do. Rather, his only focus is to be on loving his wife as Christ loved the church—that is, sacrificially.

In practical terms, this could mean, among other things, volunteering to bathe the kids or massage his wife's feet, turning off the football game and talking with her, or going shopping with her—even after he's put in a 12-hour day at work.

Sacrificial love involves participating in something that is important or a favorite of hers, even if it's relatively unimportant to you or definitely not one of your favorites. It may mean doing any of the following (although it's not limited to any or all of them):

- Initiating prayer with her without concern that your prayers may be briefer and more bottom-line than hers
- Learning to say these three phrases: "You were right," "I was wrong" and "I am sorry"
- Calling her when there is any delay in plans
- Practicing Proverbs 31:28-29 (praising her) consistently
- Accepting her communication style and opinions as different from yours, and not necessarily wrong

- Accepting her femaleness and celebrating the differences that come from it
- Asking for her opinion
- Discovering the uniqueness of her personality in order to understand her and communicate better
- Asking what TV show or movie she would like to watch

THE LEADERSHIP THAT GOD SUPPORTS

The issue of the man's leadership in the home has been a concern for years. Book after book has been written on this subject, including *Passive Men, Wild Women* and *Husbands Who Won't Lead and Wives Who Won't Follow*. We're talking about biblical headship—specifically the authority of the man to lead.

A man's motives for leading a marriage spiritually can sometimes be diluted by personal reasons, but when he allows God to lead him, and when his heart is open to God and His purposes, then his headship receives God's support.

So what does that kind of leadership look like in practical terms?

Serve

The authority God gives men to lead is built on service. This is a difficult balancing and juggling act for many. The problem is not with the teaching of male leadership, but with the man who misuses the teaching that he is to lead so that he can serve his own needs and desires. Some men behave like drill sergeants, snapping out orders at their wives and children, which doesn't reflect Scripture, but their own selfishness and insecurity.

The truth is, a husband is called to think of others—particularly his wife—first, ahead of himself. That's not easy for many men. For one thing, the idea of being a servant-leader runs counter to the thinking of our present-day "me" culture. But with some hard work and sacrifice, it can be done.

I've seen both kinds of leadership. I've seen the self-appointed "dictators" who distort scriptural teaching for their own benefit. The result of this kind of leadership is that marriages and families suffer and fragment. But I've also observed men who are servant-leaders whose families flourished as a result.

Love

God's script also calls the husband to be not just a servant-leader but also a lover, meaning that his headship of his family is not to exhibit dominating control but the sacrificial love of Jesus.

And how did Christ love when He was on earth? He was single-minded in His mission of love as He spent time with the disciples where they were weak. He defended the disciples, praised them before others and revealed Himself to them. And why did Jesus do these things? He was concerned about the church's wellbeing and future glory.

That is how a husband is to love his wife. A husband represents Jesus in the home, and his role is to bring out God's glory in his wife and lift her up—for *her* wellbeing. That is leadership that leaves a wife feeling special, valued and loved.

So how specifically can a husband do that? There are many ways; one of the most important is a husband's putting his wife first over children, parents, siblings, work, TV and hobbies. Doing this will strengthen a marriage. Conversely, not doing it will weaken a marriage.

Another thing a loving husband can do is learn his wife's "love language"—in other words, the ways she tends to hear, express and receive love from others—and package his love in a way that speaks to her and meets her needs.

We are also to love our wives unconditionally, the same way God loves all of us. We're not to love her "because she . . ." but "regardless." When you love your wife sacrificially and unconditionally, she will more fully realize God's love and regard for her, and this in turn brings glory to Him.[4]

God expects us to care for one another. A husband who neglects or demeans his wife robs her of what God wants for her and robs himself of growth and development as well.

Regarding couples caring for one another, Bryan Chapell wrote:

> Because two people who marry are to be one, if either part damages, demoralizes or degrades the other, then neither will be completely whole. Just as a basketball deflated on only one side still cannot fulfill its purposes, so a marriage with one side diminished will deprive both persons of fully being and doing what God desires. God has designed the similarities and differences of a man and woman in marriage to complement and support the spiritual growth of both. Neither part to the marriage can develop fully if either one is denied his or her personal potential.[5]

What an opportunity you and I have! It's very much like Jesus' redemptive work on behalf of the church in that a husband is not to live for himself, but should live to be used as a channel of God's goodness in his wife's life. We're to respond, react, speak and think toward her in ways that enable her to develop who she is and to develop her gifts as a way to bring glory to God.[6]

An encouraging man does this. He's a man who sincerely tells his wife, "I believe in you," "Go for it" and "How can I help you?" We are to do everything in what the Bible calls the "fullness of Jesus Christ," and that includes being married. Colossians 3:15-17 instructs us how we can equip ourselves with that fullness:

> Let the peace of Christ rule in your hearts, since as members of one body you were called to peace. And be thankful. Let the word of Christ dwell in you richly as you teach and admonish one another with all wisdom, and as you sing psalms, hymns and spiritual songs with gratitude in your hearts to God. And whatever you do, whether in word or deed, do it all in the name of the Lord Jesus, giving thanks to God the Father through Him.

LETTING CHRIST LEAD THROUGH YOU

Let's take a more detailed look at what living in the fullness of Christ means.

Let the peace of Christ rule. This could be paraphrased, "Let the peace of Christ be umpire in your heart amidst the conflicts of life. Let Christ's peace within be your counselor and decide for you what is right." The peace described here is not just the peace you feel when you have conflict. It is a sense of wholeness and wellbeing, a sense that God is in control and guiding you.

Who or what rules in your life? The indwelling peace of Christ is indispensable when it comes to blessing your spouse and bringing out God's glory.

Let the Word of Christ dwell in you. How do we allow God's Word to take up residence in us? By reading it, studying it and memorizing it.

I've seen angry people, frustrated people, anxious people and obnoxious people changed because of the power of God's Word dwelling in them. God's Word has the power to change any of us, and it has the power to bring out the best in a marriage.

When you read the Bible, ask the Holy Spirit to make it part of your life. A chapel speaker I once heard at Westmont College said, "If you take one chapter from the Word of God and read it out loud every day for a month, it will be yours for life." He was right. It works.

Do all in the name of the Lord Jesus. Everything we as Christians do—good or bad—is a reflection of Jesus Christ. Our obedient, loving behavior in our marriage reflects His presence for all the world to see. But when we react and respond in a way that is contrary to what is in the Scriptures, and contrary to our relationship with Jesus, it reflects that He does not fully occupy our life.

Paul's command to do all in the name of the Lord Jesus follows a series of commands in Colossians 3:5-14. He warns us about behaviors we are to put off because they do not reflect a person who knows Jesus Christ. He tells us to get rid of sexual immorality, impurity, lust, evil desires, greed, anger, rage, malice, slander, filthy language, and lying (see vv. 5-9), because none of these behaviors reflects the presence of Christ in our life. When we engage in any of these things, we've rewritten the script. Ridding ourselves of them will prepare us to do all in the name of Christ.

We are called to replace these negative behaviors with words and deeds that clearly exemplify that we know Christ: We are to reflect compassion, kindness, humility, gentleness, patience and forgiveness (see vv. 10-14).

The Bible says, "Husbands, likewise, dwell with them *with understanding*, giving *honor* to the wife, as to the weaker vessel, and as being *heirs together* of the grace of life, that your *prayers may not be hindered*" (1 Pet. 3:7, *NKJV*, emphasis added).

Part of dwelling with your wife *with understanding* means recognizing that your wife is in need of your covering—your protection and love. And because you are *heirs together* of God's grace, you need to *honor* her in your thoughts, words and actions. When you don't, your *prayers are hindered*. This means *all* of your prayers, not just those for your wife. Many men have not seen answers to their prayers because they have not learned this key step. One of the best ways to honor your wife is to pray for her from a heart that is clean before God.[7]

In the Bible, God commands, "All of you be of *one mind*, having *compassion* for one another; *love* as brothers, be *tenderhearted*, be *courteous*" (1 Pet. 3:8, *NKJV*, emphasis added). Paying heed to these five directives can change your life and your marriage and make you the man and husband God wants you to be.

FIVE DIRECTIVES FROM GOD

1. Be of One Mind

It's horrible to have strife in a marriage. It makes us miserable. It affects every area of our life. And it's probably the closest thing to hell we'll ever know on earth. If it goes on long enough, it can destroy everything.

2. Be Compassionate

Have you ever seen your wife suffering, but you don't know what to do about it? Some men become impatient. Others feel so at a loss or overwhelmed by it that it causes them to withdraw. If you recognize that happening to you, ask God to give you a heart of compassion. To be compassionate toward your wife is to have a deep sympathy for any area in which she suffers and to have a strong desire to alleviate that suffering.

3. Be Loving

Jesus loves us with fidelity, purity, constancy and passion, no matter how imperfect we are. If a man doesn't love his wife in the same way, he will abuse his authority and his headship, and as a result will abuse *her*. Because you are one with your wife, you must treat her the way you would your own body. You have no idea how much your love means to your wife. Don't withhold it from her, or one way or another you will lose her.

4. Be Tenderhearted

Is there anything about your wife that bothers you? Is there something that she does or says, or *doesn't* do or say, that irritates you? Do you find yourself wanting to change something about her? What happens when you try to *make* those changes occur? Rather than be impatient with your wife's weaknesses, ask God to give you a tender heart so you can pray about them. Ask Him to show you how her weaknesses are a complement to your strengths.

5. Be Courteous

Do you ever talk to your wife in a way that would be considered rude if you were speaking to a friend or business associate?

Are you kind to everyone all day at work, but then you take out your frustration, exhaustion and anger on your wife when you get home? Do you ever allow criticism of your wife to come out of your mouth in front of other people?

Marriage is hard enough without one of the parties being rude, cruel or inconsiderate. Nothing makes a marriage feel more like hell on earth. Nothing is more upsetting, defeating, tormenting, suffocating or provokes the emotions; nothing does more to bring out the worst in us than a marriage where one of the partners is lacking in common courtesy.

Praying about these five simple biblical directives will transform your life and your marriage. No matter how great your marriage is, God wants it to be better. Because God tells us to "be transformed," there is always room for improvement (Rom. 12:2).[8]

Now, having said all that, how do you see these positive qualities of unity, compassion, love, tenderheartedness and courtesy reflected in *your* marriage relationship?[9]

DISCOVER THE ENCOURAGER IN YOU

1. What have you learned from the chapter about your calling as a husband?

2. What does it mean to be an image-bearer of God in your marriage?

3. What, if anything, surprised you about how God defines leadership in marriage?

4. What is your action plan to be a better leader of your family? Describe.

5. How will you pray for your wife?

7

Questions
Men Ask

**OVER A PERIOD OF MANY YEARS, I'VE HAD NUMEROUS DISCUS-
SIONS WITH MEN ABOUT MARRIAGE.** I wish I'd made a list of all
the questions and concerns they've asked me. There are a few
concerns I've heard again and again that we'll address here.
That's what this chapter is about. Three issues stand out that
have an effect on your relationship with your wife as well as
helping to bring out the best in her.

QUESTION #1

Why don't we men ask for suggestions from our wives?

Part of the reason is that men look at the facts and usually ignore the element that women focus on—the human dimension.
Women like to figure out how their decisions will affect not
only themselves but also those around them. They enjoy eval-
uating numerous possibilities as well as reflecting upon their
feelings. They enjoy asking questions, gathering information
and searching for solutions. Because of their concern for others,
after they make a decision, they may agonize, "Was it the right
decision or not?" "What if it hurts others, or someone doesn't
approve?" Usually when a man makes a decision, it's been cast
in cement. Does any of this sound familiar yet?

Women seek the opinions of others more than men do.
They enjoy including others in the decision-making process,
whereas a man deals with a situation within the privacy of his
mind and then consults others. If he receives favorable feed-

back, he moves ahead. If not, he'll reconsider. He rarely asks for help—in any arena—because he wants to feel self-sufficient.

A classic example of this is the man who drives somewhere and gets lost. You know what I'm talking about. A wife will suggest stopping at the nearest gas station or making a phone call to get directions or checking the car's GPS if it's available. To the man, this means admitting he's out of control and can't solve his own problem. To him this feels like failure. If he does stop for help, who usually goes in and asks for assistance? You guessed it, his wife.

Feeling out of control is one of the main causes of stress in a man's life. Consider some of the other sources of stress, based on our feeling out of control:

- We are stressed when we're forced to ride in the passenger seat rather than have control of the automobile. I felt that especially when Joyce drove.
- We're stressed when we have to wait for a table at a restaurant or in line for a movie. So what do we do to reduce this stress? We frequently choose to forego the meal or movie to regain our sense of choice.
- We get infuriated by road construction and exasperated at "stupid" drivers who distract or detain us, especially those using cell phones or putting on makeup (or both at the same time!).
- We dread funerals and therapy, and sometimes equate the two as depressing reminders of life's uncertainties and our own frailty.
- We postpone dental and doctor appointments or other procedures that require us to put ourselves in others' hands.

- We're terrified of illness or injury that may interfere with our ability to be in charge of our daily life.
- We prefer requests to demands, and free choice to requests—and we'll demonstrate this by saying no to demands for things we might have actually enjoyed. (I hate this one. It's too convicting—I've done it!)
- We prefer dogs as pets over cats because dogs are more responsive and can be controlled. Cats are independent and get into power struggles with us.[1]

There's another reason we men tend not to ask for suggestions. Most men dislike being wrong, being told they are wrong, even considering they might be wrong, or the worst scenario of all, discovering their wife knew they were wrong before they did! For most men, it's the ultimate in feeling helpless and humiliated. (I've seen exceptions to this based on the security a man finds through a personal relationship with Jesus Christ, allowing Christ to refine the man's attitudes and beliefs.)

To sum it up, we men are afraid of being wrong. Fear makes us expect the worst, misinterpret what others say and act overly defensive. When a wife offers unsolicited advice or suggestions, often it's not perceived as helpful. If a wife says, "Oh, not that way, honey, try it this way instead," many men hear it as, "That's the wrong way. Can't you figure it out?" When she suggests stopping and asking for directions, he hears, "Dummy! How could you get lost? You can't even figure this out."

Because of our defensive filters, husbands and wives often hear something different from what was actually said. It's not so much a matter of being right or wrong as it is a lack of understanding. Marriage provides the opportunity for education, clarification and refinement.

One husband told me, "During the first five years of marriage, I was defensive when Mary made suggestions or gave me any feedback. One evening, when we were out to dinner, she asked me, 'What do you hear me say when I give you a suggestion or some advice?' I thought a minute and I said, 'I guess I resist it a bit. I'm defensive ... and I think you're saying I'm wrong and I'm not doing it right.' Mary said, 'Do I use the words, "You're wrong" or "inept" or "incompetent" when I offer my suggestions?' and I said, 'No, but I guess I hear that; I guess I'm afraid of being wrong.'

"Mary went on to say, 'Could I say it in a different way to make it easier to accept?' At first I was going to say that might be the answer; but then I realized the problem was not with Mary, but with me, and I told her so. I suggested that I try not to assume she was saying or implying I was wrong. She smiled at me and said, 'That'd be great. I don't like to feel I'm wrong either ... so I have an idea of how you might feel. Perhaps we could both see the other's suggestions as an opportunity to grow and become even more proficient than we are now.' That was a great and enlightening evening for us!"

How can this information about decision-making and asking for help be useful to learn? How about talking over your decision-making styles? Encourage your wife to use her style and you affirm the positive features of it. Be willing to try your wife's style in order to understand her perspective, as well as to expand your choices. Don't interpret her questions as a challenge or as stalling. Be open to something new.

It also helps when your wife understands and accepts that you may not ask for help immediately. You like to mull it over for a while, but tell her what you're doing so she doesn't feel you're ignoring her! And if you need her help, ask her. It's a sign of strength and wisdom rather than a weakness to seek help and guidance. The book of Proverbs states:

> My son, if you will receive my words and treasure up my commandments within you, making your ear attentive to skillful and godly Wisdom, and inclining and directing your heart and mind to understanding [applying all your powers to the quest for it] (Prov. 2:1-2, *AMP*).

> Lean on, trust and be confident in the Lord with all your heart and mind and do not rely on your own insight or understanding. In all your ways know, recognize, and acknowledge Him, and He will direct and make straight and plain your paths. Be not wise in your own eyes; reverently fear and worship the Lord and turn [entirely] away from evil (Prov. 3:5-7, *AMP*).

> The way of a fool is right in his own eyes, but he who listens to counsel is wise (Prov. 12:15, *AMP*).

> He who refuses and ignores instruction and correction despises himself, but he who heeds reproof gets understanding (Prov. 15:32, *AMP*).

QUESTION 2
What if I want my wife to change in some areas?

I can think of a dozen comebacks to this question, but I thought better of them. So I'll just share a wise quote:

> We try to change people to conform to our ideas of how they should be. So does God. But there the similarity

ends. The way in which we try to get other people to con-
form is far different than the way in which God works
with us. Our ideas of what the other person should do or
how we should act may be an improvement or an impris-
onment. We may be setting the other person free of behavior patterns that are restricting his development, or we
may be simply chaining him up in another behavioral
bondage. The changes God works in us are always freeing,
freeing to become that which He has created us to be.[2]

Stop and read that again. If your request fits this, then go for
it. If not, then you know what to do.

Whatever change you want your wife to make needs to be ad-
vantageous for both you and her, as well as for the relationship.
It's not your responsibility as her husband to take on the job of
reformer. The Holy Spirit can do that much better. Your task is to
request change with your wife and provide an atmosphere of acceptance and patience that allows God freedom to work. Then
learn to trust God to do the work.

Scripture does *not* say that in order to bring about change in
another person we criticize, tear down, put down, undermine self-
esteem or find fault. Consider these Scripture passages. In fact,
read them out loud:

Do not judge and criticize and condemn others, so that
you may not be judged and criticized and condemned
yourselves. For just as you judge and criticize and condemn others, you will be judged and criticized and
condemned, and in accordance with the measure you
[use to] deal out to others, it will be dealt out again to
you (Matt. 7:1-2, *AMP*).

Then let us no more criticize and blame and pass judgment on one another, but rather decide and endeavor never to put a stumbling block or an obstacle or a hindrance in the way of a brother (Rom. 14:13, *AMP*).

Fathers, do not provoke or irritate or fret your children [do not be hard on them or harass them], lest they become discouraged and sullen and morose and feel inferior and frustrated. [Do not break their spirit.] (Col. 3:21, *AMP*).

If you're a faultfinder, you'll drive your wife away from you. Too often, legitimate requests get swallowed up by finding fault.

Here are some reasons why faultfinding is so destructive to your marriage:

Faultfinding will wound your wife. Constant verbal and nonverbal criticism says, "I don't accept you for who you are. You don't measure up, and I can't accept you until you do." In more than 40 years of counseling I've heard so many people in my office cry out in pain, "My husband's criticism rips me apart. He makes me feel like dirt. I don't feel accepted. And right now I'm still looking for someone who will tell me I'm all right." A wounded spouse becomes afraid or angry and retaliates through overt or covert withdrawal, resentment or aggression.

Faultfinding really doesn't change your wife. Why do something that doesn't work? Though she may appear to change her behavior in response to your criticism, her heart rarely changes. Some wives simply learn to cover their inner attitudes with compliance. Then resentment grows and love dies.

Guess what? Faultfinding is contagious. A fault-finding husband teaches intolerance to his wife. So both of you learn to be critical and unaccepting not only of each other, but of yourself.

Faultfinding actually reinforces negative traits and behaviors. When you pay undue attention to your wife's mistakes or even irresponsible behaviors, you tend to reinforce instead of eliminate them.

Healthy marriages have a common ingredient—mutual education. Mutual education means that both of you must become skilled teachers as well as receptive learners. The reason for this is to develop a greater degree of compatibility. If you neglect this education process, your relationship could be in jeopardy.

Mutual education is a gentle process. It involves positive modeling of the desired attitudes or behavior, gentle prodding, being sensitive—not blaming or re-buking. It focuses on the positive, and you want to manage that change so the end result is positive.[3]

I'm sure these things are what you want, too.

I've included some firsthand statements telling how change actually happened in a relationship. This is what one wife said:

I'll admit I'm not the most open person to change. But I guess I've changed quite a bit. I'd like to think it was all my decision and my choice to change, but in reality, Bill was the instigator. And part of it was that he believed I could change and he created a safe atmosphere to do some things differently. It was okay if I failed.

I had some frustrations in both business and social gatherings. I tended to be too accommodating with others and often I would end up regretting my decisions. When I talked them over in advance with Bill, he asked me a question I've now learned to ask myself, "Is this what I want at this time, what I *really* want, or what I think I should want to make others happy?" Since he worked with me on that, I've changed my responses to others.

When we went out socially, I always felt pressure to talk with everyone and make sure they were having a good time. It was really draining, and I'd come back from parties or dinners at church second-guessing myself and wishing I hadn't gone. Bill started asking me the question, "Are you having a good time? If not, why not?" during such an event and it really got me to thinking. He also asked me, "Are these people really expecting you to do all you do, or are these your own expectations?"

Sometimes those questions irritated me, but in his gentle way, Bill forced me to challenge my beliefs and then evaluate them. I've learned that I was making a lot of unfounded assumptions as well. Yes, I've changed, but I have to give Bill a lot of credit.

Take in the words of this husband:

Adjusting to marriage was a difficult process for my wife and me. The first three years were miserable, and we felt more like adversaries than allies. We were both on a crusade to change one another. It wasn't working. Then we decided to try an idea that we read about. We each made a list of all the things that bothered us about each other.

They weren't easy to read. In fact, reading them was more difficult than hearing them. We each read some things we had never heard before.

The next step was different but great. We put our lists in the fireplace and burned them. As we watched them burn and crumble into dead ashes, we just sat there in silence, holding hands and thinking. It had been a long time since we'd had a positive time together like that.

We then made individual lists of all the good things we could think of about each other. It wasn't easy since our focus had been on the negatives. But by the next day our lists were finished. We shared our new lists with one another and then we made a commitment to read this list and affirm one another daily for at least one of these positive traits. But it didn't end there. We posted the lists in the bedroom and continue to add to them as we discover new positive traits. Now when either of us suggests a change for the other, we're more open to considering it since it's expressed in the context of a positive relationship.

If you choose to do this, how do you think this step would impact your marriage? It's worth considering.

CREATING A CLIMATE FOR CHANGE

Let's face it. There will be times when you would like your wife to change. But what guidelines create a climate for change? Your request needs to be reasonable and attainable. In other words, is it something that's possible for your wife to change? If you want to see a basic personality change, forget it. An extrovert will always be an extrovert, and an introvert will remain an introvert. But responses can be modified.

If you want your wife's attitude to change, don't count on it. Can she change your attitude? Doubtful. If you want your wife to "feel what you feel" and feel with the same intensity, you're reaching for the impossible dream. However, you can ask for a change in behavior that can *affect* personality expression, attitudes and feelings. But your request should give you an affirmative response to the question, "Will this request enhance our relationship and create a greater depth of intimacy?" This is the fundamental purpose for change.

The authors of *Two Friends in Love* give us some guidelines:

When change is needed in our traits and personalities, it is beyond the realm of the man-inspired, man-prompted characteristics. Those that are God-given do not need touching up. They are the way they are. They only need to be acknowledged and appreciated. However, in the man-related realm, when there are characteristics that should be reworked because of the harmful effects they're having on the marriage, exercise great care in the way you handle change.[4]

To create a climate for change, you will need to be persistent and patient. You'll need to keep trying in a creative, sensitive and loving manner, even when it doesn't seem to work. And you will need to be realistic and not expect too much. That's patience.

Will your request for change help your wife as well as you? Will you both become a stronger person? Will it increase Christian growth and maturity? Or is the request not that important after all? If you ask yourself these questions, you can become a skilled teacher, and both of you can assist each other in the growth process.

When I conduct premarital counseling, I ask a number of confrontational questions. In the initial session I ask, "What passage of Scripture would you like your fiancé to implement that will make him or her an even stronger and more mature person?"

You can imagine some of the responses. About half of the individuals need a week to think about the answer. After they select a passage, I share my reason for the question. I tell them it's helpful to run a request for change through the grid of Scripture to see if the Word of God has anything to say about it. (Even if Scripture is silent on the subject, the request may still be legitimate.) Consulting Scripture can help a person refine his requests for change.

For example, if we want our spouses to change something in their character, Galatians 5:22-23 is the ultimate model of the qualities we can encourage our wives toward. We should desire the same qualities for ourselves!

But the fruit of the [Holy] Spirit [the work which His presence within accomplishes] is love, joy (gladness), peace, patience (an even temper, forbearance), kindness, goodness (benevolence), faithfulness, gentleness (meekness, humility), self-control (self-restraint, continence). Against such things there is no law [that can bring a charge] (*AMP*).

Following this passage will certainly bring out the best in each of you.

QUESTION #3

Sometimes I wonder if my wife and I are from different planets. I'll say something totally different from what she hears, even a compliment. And sometimes I don't get what she's trying to get across to me either. It didn't seem this hard when we were dating. Were we just blind and deaf then or have we changed that much, or what? Help!

Let me answer that with an experience my wife and I had several years ago. It really showed the uniqueness of men's and women's communication styles. We were visiting historical Williamsburg in Virginia, a fascinating and charming setting that preserves our colonial history. When we took the tour of the governor's mansion, the tour guide was a man. As we entered the large entry door, he began to give a factual description of the purpose of the room as well as the way it was furnished. He described in detail the various ancient guns on the wall and pointed to the unique display of flintlock rifles arranged in a circle on the rounded ceiling. When he said there were 64 of them, some originals and others replicas, I immediately began counting them (which is a typical male response—we're into numbers). The guide was knowledgeable and he gave an excellent detailed description as we went from room to room. He seemed to be quite structured and focused. I thought it was great.

We had to leave before the tour was completed to meet friends for lunch. Because we both enjoyed the presentation so much, we decided to return the next day and take the tour again. What a difference! This time our guide was a woman. We entered the same room and she said, "Now, you'll notice a few guns on the wall and ceiling, but notice the covering on these chairs and the tapestry on the walls. They are . . ." And with that she launched into a detailed description of items that had either been ignored or just given a passing mention the day before. And on it went throughout the tour.[5]

It didn't take much to figure out what was going on. It was a classic example of gender differences. The first tour guide was speaking more to men and the second guide was speaking more to women. Actually, we ended up with the best tour imaginable because we heard both perspectives. What a benefit it would be to the tourists if the guides incorporated both perspectives into their presentations!

You're not alone in your struggle with communication. For years I've asked men and women in seminar settings to identify what frustrates them about the communication style of the opposite sex. Here's a listing of some of the women's responses:

They don't share their feelings or emotions enough. It's like they grew up emotionally handicapped.

They seem to go into a trance when they're watching sports or when I bring up certain subjects. They're not able to handle more than one task or subject at a time.

Men seem to think they can do things better, even when they can't, and they won't take any advice, even if it helps them.

They don't listen well. They're always trying to fix our problems.

Men need more intuition—get off the factual bandwagon.

Men need to learn to enjoy shopping like we do. They just don't know what they're missing.

Men need more sensitivity, concern, compassion and empathy.

I wish men weren't so threatened by women's ideas and perspectives.

They're so over-involved in their work and career. They want a family but they don't get involved.

Sex—that's the key word. Don't they think about anything else? They're like a microwave oven. Push the buttons and they're cookin'. Their on button is never off.

Here are some other responses that were recorded in a group setting:

Men think too much. There's more to life than thinking.

I wish he didn't think he always had to define everything. I feel as if I've been talking to a dictionary. Every week for the past year my husband has said, "What do you mean? I can't talk to you if I don't understand your words. Give me some facts, not those darn feelings!" Well, sometimes I can't give him facts and definitions. Man shall not live by definitions alone!

I don't think men understand the difference between sharing their feelings and what they think about their feelings. They tend to intellectualize so much of the time. Why do men have to think about how they feel? Just come out with it unedited. He doesn't have to respond like a textbook or edit everything he shares. I wonder if the emotional side of a man threatens him? Of course you can't always control your emotional responses. So what?

My husband is an engineer, and you ought to be around when his engineer friends come over. The house is like a cerebral, cognitive conference! All logical facts. They walk in with their slide rulers and calculators, and it's as though the house were swept clean of any emotional response. They talk, but they don't disclose. They share, but on the surface. They're safe and secure. Sometimes I have this urge to come into the room and start sharing emotions with all sorts of emotional words and then start crying to see how long it would take for some of them to bolt out the door, jump out the window or hide their faces behind a magazine. Why, I could even threaten 10 men inside of a minute. I never realized what power I had. I think I'll do that next time they're over.

What about men? What frustrates them about women? It's generally the opposite of what women say frustrates them about men. Here's what the men said about women in this survey.

They're too emotional. They need to be more logical.

How can they spend so much time talking? When it's said, it's said. So many of them are expanders. I wish they would get to the bottom line quicker and at least identify the subject!

They're too sensitive. They're always getting their feelings hurt.

Why do they cry so easily? It doesn't make sense to me.

I think most women are shopaholics. Their eyes glaze over when they see a shopping mall.

They're so changeable. I wish they'd make up their minds and then keep them made up.

Maybe they think we can read minds, but we can't. I don't think they can either.

What's wrong with the sex drive? Sex is great, only they don't have that much interest. It takes forever to get them interested.

They think they have the spiritual gift of changing men. They ought to quit. We can't be fixed and we don't need to be.

They're so involved with other people and their problems.

Women are moody and negative. You can't satisfy them.

I wish they would leave some things alone. They're always trying to fix something that isn't broken.

Here are some additional responses men have shared in seminars:

> I understand her need to talk about us and our relationship. I happen to think there is a right way and a wrong way to talk about things. If you're not careful, the whole thing can get out of hand. It's best to be as rational as possible. If you let it get too emotional, you never can make any good decisions, and if it gets too personal, someone could get hurt. A little bit of distance goes a long way where a lot of these things are concerned.

> It's important, first, to set out clearly what the issues are. I don't think women do this very well. They latch on to the first thing that comes to mind, and get totally emotionally involved in it. The next thing you know, you're arguing about everything under the sun, and no one is happy. I believe in a clear definition of the problem at the outset. If she can tell me exactly what is bothering her, we can deal with it logically. If she can't do that, then there's no sense even talking about it.

As we consider some of the unique characteristics of men and women, let's keep two things in mind. First, there are some generalizations that pertain to men and women. But there will always be exceptions in varying degrees. Second, the characteristics unique to men and to women are not negative. It is *not* a fault to be either way. Some of the characteristics will be more pronounced in some people because of personality type as well as upbringing. The problem arises when people feel they are always right or that the way they do things is the only right way. They don't care about understanding and accepting the opposite sex the way they are. The more flexibility a person develops, the more his or her marriage will benefit.[6] And your wife will feel understood and encouraged.

Getting Fluent in a New Language

Let's go further in this communication process. When you communicate with your wife, realize that you're talking with a foreigner, and both of you need to learn one another's language. It's as though you each have a secret code that the other needs to decipher.

I was at a board meeting for a university, and one of the guest lecturers for a marriage conference was Dr. Emerson Eggericks, author of *Love and Respect*. In the few minutes he had to speak to us, he talked about those gender differences. A husband and wife can make the same identical statement but mean two totally different things. For example, if you're going to an event, and you hear your wife say, "I don't have a thing to wear," do you believe that? Do you take it literally? Is that what she really means? What about you? If you said, "I don't have a thing to wear," what does that mean?

A woman's statement, "I don't have a thing to wear," usually means, "I don't have anything *new* to wear or that I want to wear"; whereas your statement usually means, "I don't have anything *clean* to wear." I'm sure you could come up with a list of words and phrases that you both use with different meanings. Clarifying what you mean and asking clarifying questions of your wife will do wonders for the communication process.

Men and women have very different approaches to communication. When a man starts a conversation, it is generally because he perceives there is a problem. If there is no perceived problem, he feels no particular need to talk. His wife, on the other hand, has a constant desire to talk with her husband. She wants to connect him to everything in her life and assumes he wants to connect her to everything in his life.

"Connect" with Me

When your wife begins a conversation with you, assume that she needs to connect the issues of her life together. She doesn't need you to work your male logic into her thinking process. She simply needs you to help her make the connections. That's all. Assist her, not fix her. You will do well if you view the conversation as a journey she is going to lead you on. Pack your bags, go on the journey and encourage her to take the conversation wherever she wants. Many men refuse to do this because they are afraid that if they give their wives permission to talk until they are done, the end will never come. This just isn't true. Most men don't know this, however, because they have never helped their wives finish a conversation.

Your wife is driven to connect. Because she is aware of all the issues of her life, and because it is impossible to fix every issue in her life all at once, she approaches things differently than you. Before she looks for solutions, she interacts with each part of her life and experiences the appropriate emotion of each issue. Things she should be upset with, she gets upset about. Things that are sentimental bring soft words and flowing tears. Things that are exciting bring giggles and enthusiasm. Things that are intense bring focused concentration. Each issue gets its own emotional reaction. That is why she can experience such a range of emotions in one conversation. Just because you, as a man, cannot keep up with her does not mean that your way is better. If you are willing to serve this need of hers, you'll be married to a much happier woman. You'll know when she is done connecting things together because she'll let out a deep sigh and may say something like, "You understand me like no one else in the world" or "You are my best friend. Thanks." You may not really understand what she is going through, but it will definitely make her life better.

A common complaint from men is that their wives ramble on ... and on ... and on ... and on seemingly with no point. Because the man cannot figure out where the conversation is going, he feels powerless to do anything about it. A sense of failure sets in, and he concludes that his wife is unreasonable and unable to think through issues.

A new perspective is needed. Men, to help you understand your wife's need to finish conversations, imagine if everything in your life ended early. What if you were never able to finish a meal because it was taken away from you when you were halfway through? What if every sporting event you watched on TV was turned off five minutes before the end of the game? What if every sexual encounter ended before its climax? What if every project you started had to be abandoned before you were able to finish it? How are you feeling? Can you sense the frustration and irritation this would bring? If life were actually like this, your anger would always be close to the surface, and your motivation to keep pursuing these activities would be shattered.

This is the way your wife feels when she's not able to finish conversations with you. She experiences the same frustration and irritation. Her motivation to keep talking is threatened but her need to talk with you won't go away. She builds up hope that this time you will be interested, only to have it shattered by your insistence on getting to the point. The game has ended early, and the project must be left unfinished and unattended. You can avoid this irritating chain of events by simply taking some time to listen to your wife on a regular basis. She will keep things more connected, and your life will be easier.[7]

One of the greatest gifts you will ever give to your wife is communication—the kind both of you can understand. Think about this: Communication is to love what blood is to the body. Without it, there's no relationship. It may be helpful to review some principles of communication.

The Word of God is the most effective resource for learning to communicate. In it you will find a workable pattern for healthy relationships. Here are just a few of the guidelines it offers:

- "Some people like to make cutting remarks, but the words of the wise soothe and heal" (Prov. 12:18, *TLB*).
- "Pride leads to arguments; be humble, take advice and become wise" (Prov. 13:10, *TLB*).
- "A wise man controls his temper. He knows that anger causes mistakes" (Prov. 14:29, *TLB*).
- "Gentle words cause life and health; griping brings discouragement. . . . Everyone enjoys giving good advice, and how wonderful it is to be able to say the right thing at the right time!" (Prov. 15:4,23, *TLB*).
- "Love forgets mistakes; nagging about them parts the best of friends" (Prov. 17:9, *TLB*).
- "Timely advice is as lovely as golden apples in a silver basket" (Prov. 25:11, *TLB*).
- "A friendly discussion is as stimulating as the sparks that fly when iron strikes iron" (Prov. 27:17, *TLB*).

- "We take our lead from Christ, who is the source of everything we do. He keeps us in step with each other" (Eph. 4:15-16, *THE MESSAGE*).
- "A man who refuses to admit his mistakes can never be successful. But if he confesses and forsakes them, he gets another chance" (Prov. 28:13, *TLB*).
- "Watch the way you talk. Let nothing foul or dirty come out of your mouth. Say only what helps, each word a gift" (Eph. 4:29, *THE MESSAGE*).
- "Let all bitterness and wrath and anger and clamor and slander be put away from you, along with all malice. Be kind to one another, tender-hearted, forgiving each other, just as God in Christ also has forgiven you" (Eph. 4:31-32, *NASB*).
- "For we all stumble in many ways. If anyone does not stumble in what he says, he is a perfect man, able to bridle the whole body as well" (Jas. 3:2, *NASB*).
- "Let him who means to love life and see good days refrain his tongue from evil and his lips from speaking guile" (1 Pet. 3:10, *AMP*, author's paraphrase).

If these behaviors are evident in your marriage, you will be bringing out the best in your wife.

"CHERISH" IS THE WORD

I have one last suggestion, which has not only saved a number of marriages from disaster, but has also taken marriages from a "so-so" level to "this is a great marriage." The principle here in many ways fulfills many of the scriptural guidelines suggested in this book.

Over the years, I have used a pattern for increasing positive behaviors for couples in both counseling and in seminars. I've talked about it and written about it before. It goes by various names, such as "caring behaviors" or "cherishing behaviors." Let me present it in a way so that you can do it for yourself.

Ask each other the question, "What would you like me to do for you to show how much I care for you?" The answer must be positive, specific and something that can be performed daily. The purpose of each action must be to increase positive behavior, not to decrease negative behavior. For example:

- "Please greet me with a hug and a kiss" is positive.
- "Don't ignore me so much" is negative.
- "Please line the children's bikes along the back wall of the garage when you come home" is more specific and thus better than, "please train the children to keep their bikes in the proper place."

Ted would like Sue "to sit next to him on the sofa when they listen to the news after dinner." This is positive and specific. It's better than asking her to "stop being too preoccupied and distant" (a negative and overly general request).

Sue would like Ted "to kiss her good-bye when they part in the morning." This is positive and specific, which is different from "stop being so distant and cold" (a negative and overly general response).

GROUND RULES FOR "CHERISH" REQUESTS

Avoid making vague comments by writing down beforehand your answers to the question, "What would you like me to do for you to show how much I care for you?"

The small, cherishing behaviors *must not concern past conflicts*. Your requests must not be old demands. That is, the requests must not concern any subject over which you have quarreled. The behaviors must be those that can be done on an everyday basis. The behaviors must also be minor ones—those that can be done easily.

These requests should, as much as possible, be something only your wife can fulfill. If they're things that a hired hand could perform, they may create problems. For example, if they're mostly task-oriented, like "wash the car," "take out the trash," "clean out the camper," "have the dishes and house all cleaned up by the time I get home," and so on, they don't reflect intimacy and the building of your personal relationship. Some better responses would be, "Ask me what excites me about my new job," or "Turn out the lights and let's sit holding hands without talking," or "Rub my back for five minutes."

Each list can include 15 to 18 items. Listing as many as 18 creates more interest and makes it easier to follow through with requests. When you give your lists to each other, the only discussion you may carry on about the list is to ask for clarification if it is needed.

Your commitment is to do at least two items on your wife's caring list each day, whether or not she is doing any positive behaviors on your list. I know it sounds unfair, but you can do it.

Here are some suggestions for the "caring" lists:

1. Say "hello" to me and kiss me in the morning when we wake up.
2. Say "goodnight" to me.
3. Sometimes bring me home a pretty flower or leaf.

4. Call me during the day and ask, "How's it going?"
5. Put a candle on the dinner table and turn off the light.
6. Hold me when we're watching TV.
7. Leave me a surprise note.
8. Take a shower or bath with me when the kids are gone.
9. Kiss or touch me when you leave for work.
10. Tell me about your best experience during the day.
11. Hold my hand in public.
12. Tell me I'm nice to be around.
13. Praise me in front of the kids.
14. Ask me how you can pray for me.

Many of the cherishing behaviors you request of your wife may seem unimportant or even trivial. Some may be a bit embarrassing because at first they may seem artificial. That's all right. These small behaviors can set the tone of your relationship. They are the primary building blocks for a fulfilling marriage. They establish an environment of positive expectations and change a negative mindset. I don't know any couple that doesn't want that.

When the lists are completed, exchange them with each other. Discuss the cherishing behaviors you have requested. Don't be hesitant about telling your wife how you would like to have the cherishing behaviors done for you.

For example: "Remember the way you used to bring me a flower when we were first married? You presented it to me when you met me at the door—after you had kissed me. It made me feel really loved."

During the discussion it is likely that both of you will think of a few more cherishing behaviors that you would enjoy receiving. Add them to the lists. The more behaviors on the lists the better. But make sure the lists are approximately equal in length.

The basic principle behind this approach is this: If you will increase your positive actions toward each other, they'll eventually crowd out and eliminate the negative. In addition, behaving in a loving, caring way will generate the habit of responding more positively and can build feelings of love.

DISCOVER THE ENCOURAGER IN YOU

1. What is more typical of you when your wife is talking—to tell her to get to the point, or encourage her to use you as a sounding board? What new insight did you learn in this chapter about a woman's style of communication?

2. When was the last time (if ever) that your wife thanked you for listening to her entire story without interrupting or trying to "fix" any concern she shared?

3. Think back to conversations that have made a difference in your relationship with your wife, for better or for worse. What specific words or phrases came up repeatedly when you spoke to your wife in a negative way; what words or phrases came up when you spoke to her in a positive way?

4. Review the 13 bulleted Scripture passages that are guidelines for communicating with others. Which verse or

verses speak most strongly to you? What words, phrases or behaviors do you need to ask God to help you give up?

5. What requests of your wife would you write on your "Cherish List"?

8

The Power of a
Praying Man

A YOUNG WIFE IN MY OFFICE WAS ANIMATED BUT NOT UPSET. "I never dreamed that what has happened in our marriage during the past year was possible," she said. "We've gone along for years just sort of ho-hum. Nothing bad, nothing spectacular—just steady. I guess we were in a rut. It was comfortable, and I guess we felt, or I did, that this was the way it would always be. But Jim came home from that men's conference and made all kinds of changes. Even though they were mostly positive, it took me awhile to adjust.

"The first thing he did was come up to me and apologize for not telling me that he prayed for me every day and had for years. How would I have ever known? In fact, that's what I started to say, but I caught myself and thanked him for telling me. A week later, he 'casually' asked me how I would feel about praying together and reading from the Bible occasionally. I have to laugh now because it's like he wanted me to but wasn't sure how I would respond. So we did.

"I can't explain why or what happened, but there is this incredible sense of bonding or closeness now that we never had before. We pray, we read, we share. Sometimes I call him and pray a sentence prayer for him over the phone. Others have seen our relationship change. And when they ask, we tell them. I guess we're finally experiencing what the Bible says about cleaving, in the full sense of the word."

What happened to this couple?

We could call it spiritual bonding, spiritual intimacy or spiritual closeness. Whatever it is, it really brought out the best.

What if I asked you, "How close are you spiritually as a couple?" What would you say? Usually there are two responses: (1) "We're not spiritually close" or "We're not as close as we could be"; or (2) "I think we'd like to be." Many couples, when they finally talk about it, discover they would like to be closer spiritually, but they were uncomfortable dealing with it. It was difficult, so it was never discussed. Has that been your experience?

I often hear couples say, "We need to; we want to." What keeps you from developing this area of spiritual togetherness that can bring an even greater depth to the other dimensions of intimacy?

Some say, "We really don't know any couples who do this, and we're not exactly sure how to go about it." Perhaps there is a lack of role models to follow because we don't ask others what they do. We would be embarrassed if asked, so we feel others would be as well. And we avoid putting them on the spot.

Still others say, "We just don't have time. With our schedules we hardly have enough time to say hello to each other, let alone have devotions together."

To relate together spiritually means creatively meshing your schedules. And yet, we have the greatest time-saving gadgets. I'm going to be blunt here: When someone says they don't have time to develop spiritual intimacy in their marriage, I say, "I don't agree. I've never met anyone who couldn't work out the time. It may take some creative juggling, but it's a choice—like so much of the rest of life. You have to be flexible, committed and have realistic expectations for what you want to have happen in the relationship."

Others have said, "We're not at the same place spiritually in order to share this together." Perhaps praying or reading the Bible together would help you become more unified spiritually.

Some husbands have simply asked, "Why? Why develop this? Why do this? I'm not sure of the benefits." If a man says this to me, I won't even debate the issue with him or try to convince him. But I can say this: "I don't know if anyone could really explain why or convince you. Perhaps the best way to discover the benefits of what I'm saying is to try it for a week. Then evaluate the process to see if it does anything for you. Anyone can give one week of his or her life for an experiment such as this."

I know that a man can have a strong personal relationship with the Lord, but never invite his partner into his life to experience the spiritual journey together. When one partner wants this and the other resists overtly or just drags his or her feet, it can have a damaging effect on the relationship.

A friend of mine shared his experience before he and his wife decided to develop this dimension in their relationship:

When it came to the day-to-day sharing of our own spiritual journeys (the real test of spiritual maturity), it wasn't there.

Jan would want us to read something together, and I would be too busy. She would want us to pray, and I would be too tired. She would share something deeply personal, but I would not respond. I would listen intently, but my sympathetic stares were met with deafening silence. On the rare occasions when I did respond, it was only with a summarization of what she had said, an acknowledgment, but never a personal reflection.

To Jan, my avoidant behavior communicated that I was not interested in spiritual matters and, to some extent, that I did not care about her needs. Gradually, my excuses and my silence took their toll, and she tired of her efforts. The requests for my involvement, the statements of her need, the times of her own personal sharing—all tapered off. Jan seemed to resign herself to the fact that it just was not going to happen. For whatever reason, we were not going to be spiritually intimate. Our sharing would be limited to crises.

With Jan's resignation came some resentment. This was not a seething caldron type of problem, but on occasion it would become clear that "resignation" had not brought "resolution." Jan still desired the closeness that was missing, and the disappointment was frustrating.[1]

This story is so typical. Many of us avoid this area. Why? It's uncomfortable. We don't feel competent or capable. We'd rather be private about our spiritual life. Sometimes we may feel that our wife prays better than we do.

Many a couple feels close to their partner in every way except spiritually. In that area they feel isolated. But often this isolation can't be kept in check, and it may creep into other areas of a couple's life and impact those areas too. The more one person wants to be close spiritually, and the other resists, the more resentment will build.

Many couples find themselves in this bind, but it can be overcome.

WHAT IS INTIMACY?

Intimacy suggests a very strong personal relationship, a special emotional closeness that includes understanding and being understood by someone who is very special.

Intimacy means taking the risk to be close to someone and allowing that someone to step inside your personal boundaries. Sometimes intimacy can hurt. As you lower your defenses to let your wife close, you reveal the real, intimate, secret you to her, which includes your weaknesses and faults. With the real you exposed, you become vulnerable to possible ridicule from her. The risk of pain is there, but the rewards of intimacy greatly overshadow the risk. Believe me, I know.

Although intimacy means vulnerability, it also means security. Openness can be scary, but the acceptance each of you offers in the midst of vulnerability provides a wonderful sense of security. Intimate couples can feel safe and accepted—fully exposed perhaps, yet fully accepted.

It's impossible for a meaningful marriage to exist without intimacy. If you don't know how your wife thinks and feels about various issues or concerns, she is somewhat of a stranger to you.

It's often assumed that intimacy automatically occurs between married partners. But I've seen far too many "married strangers." I've talked to too many husbands and wives who feel isolated from their spouses and lonely, even after many years of marriage. I've heard statements like:

"We share the same house, the same table, and the same bed, but we might as well be strangers."

"We've lived together for 23 years, and yet I don't know my spouse any better now than when we married."

"What really hurts is that we can spend a weekend together and I still feel lonely. I think I married someone who would have preferred being a hermit in some ways."

No, intimacy is not automatic. Actually, there are several dimensions of intimacy. It's not limited to one area of marriage, such as sex. Several elements are involved in creating an intimate relationship. Many marriages have gaps in them for one reason or another. You may be close in two or three areas but distant in others. If you think you have a close, intimate relationship, but you're distant in a couple of them or in each, there's work to be done. Let's consider the various dimensions before looking at the spiritual aspect, because they all relate.

Emotional intimacy is the foundation for relating in a couple's relationship. This isn't easy for most men. There's a sense of closeness when this exists. You share everything in the emotional arena, including your hurts and your joys. You understand each other and you're attentive to your wife's feelings. But this takes work for most men.

Social intimacy involves having friends in common rather than always socializing separately. Having mutual friends to play with, talk with, pray with and give reciprocal support to is reflective of this important dimension.

Sexual intimacy is taken for granted in marriage. Many couples have sex but no sexual intimacy. Performing a physical act is one thing, but communicating about it is another. Sexual intimacy involves satisfaction with what occurs. But it also means you talk about it, endeavor to meet your wife's needs and keep it from becoming routine. There's an understanding of each other's unique gender needs, and flexibility in meeting them.

There is even the dimension of *intellectual intimacy*—the sharing of ideas and the stimulation of each other's level of knowledge and understanding. You are each different, and you have grown because of what your partner has shared with you.

Joyce and I became much more involved in this way in the last 20 years of our marriage. We shared or pointed out some idea or saved something we learned in an article, book, newscast or TV program. We valued each other's opinion. But for this dimension to exist, you need mutual respect. You can't be threatened by the sharing, but must value what's given.

Recreational intimacy means you share and enjoy the same interests and activities. You just like to play together, and it doesn't have to be competitive. You have fun together, and it draws you closer together.

Then we come to *spiritual intimacy*. To keep everything in balance, and to be complete, you also need the other kinds of intimacy. I've seen some couples who have spiritual intimacy but lack social and recreational. That's out of balance.[2]

CREATING SPIRITUAL INTIMACY

I know couples who worship regularly together, but there is no spiritual intimacy. I know couples who regularly read the Scriptures together but have no spiritual intimacy. I know couples who pray and share together but are lacking in spiritual intimacy. I know some couples who don't pray and share, yet they have spiritual intimacy.

What makes the difference? It seems to be their attitudes. Spiritual intimacy is a heart's desire to be close to God and submit to His direction for your lives. It is the willingness to seek His guidance together, to allow the teaching of His Word in your everyday life. It's a willingness to allow God to help you over-come your sense of discomfort over sharing spiritually and learn to see your marriage together as a spiritual adventure. It's a will-ingness to put Jesus Christ as Lord of your lives and to look to Him for direction in your decisions, such as which house to buy, where to go on vacations or which school is best for the chil-dren. He will direct both of you and change your hearts to be in agreement rather than speak just through one of you.

Spiritual intimacy in marriage requires both partners to submit to the leadership and lordship of Christ, instead of com-peting for control. One author wrote:

> We can gather all the facts needed in making a decision. We can thresh out our differences as to the shape and direction our decision should take. We can put off the decision while we allow the relevant information to simmer in our minds. Even then, however, we may be uneasy: we still don't know what is best to do, and the right decisions just won't come.
>
> When we turn to the Lord Jesus Christ and open our consciences to His Spirit's leading, some new events, remembrances and forgotten facts will come to us. A whole new pattern will emerge. We can then move with abandon in a whole new direction that we had not pre-viously considered. Looking back, we may conclude that God's providence delivered us from what would have been the worst possible decision. Jesus as Lord made the difference between deliverance and destruction.[3]

When Jesus is Lord of your marriage, it relieves you of the problem of experiencing a power struggle. Jesus expressed something interesting to His disciples when He said, "You know that those who are regarded as rulers of the Gentiles lord it over them, and their high officials exercise authority over them. Not so with you. Instead, whoever wants to become great among you must be your servant" (Mark 10:42-43).

I've seen marriages in which one member dictates the spiritual dimension by selecting the church to attend, the meetings attended, what magazines and books are allowed, as well as which Bible version is the accepted one! It's difficult to see how this reflects Paul's words: "Outdo one another in showing honor" (Rom. 12:10, *RSV*) to each other.

Even in a spiritually intimate marriage, faith differences may surface occasionally, but that's normal. With tolerance for diversity, couples can have a shared faith relationship that includes his faith, her faith and their faith.

Some couples seem to be able to develop spiritual intimacy, but others never do. What makes the difference? Spiritual intimacy has the opportunity to grow in a relationship that has a degree of stability. When the two of you experience trust, honesty, open communication and dependability, you are more willing to risk being vulnerable spiritually. Creating this dimension will increase the stability factor as well.

For you to have spiritual intimacy, you need shared beliefs as to who Jesus is and the basic tenets of your Christian faith. You may have different beliefs about the Second Coming of Christ, or whether all the spiritual gifts are for today or not. One of you may enjoy an informal church service while the other likes a high church formal service, or one of you may be Charismatic and the other not. It's important that your beliefs are important to you. You've made them something personal and significant for your life. There can still be spiritual intimacy within this diversity.

We hear about mismatched couples when one is a Christian and the other isn't. You can also have a mismatch when both are believers but one wants to grow and is growing, and the other doesn't and isn't![4]

A great way to encourage spiritual intimacy is to share the history of your spiritual life. Many couples know where their spouses are currently, but very little of how they came to that place. You could use the following questions to discover more about your partner's faith:

1. What did your parents believe about God, Jesus, church, prayer, the Bible?
2. What was your definition of being spiritually alive?
3. Which parent did you see as being spiritually alive?
4. What specifically did each teach you directly and indirectly about spiritual matters?
5. Where did you first learn about God? About Jesus? About the Holy Spirit? At what age?
6. What was your best experience in church as a child? As a teen?
7. What was your worst experience in church as a child? As a teen?
8. Describe your conversion experience. When? Who was involved? Where?
9. If possible, describe your baptism. What did it mean to you?
10. Which Sunday School teacher influenced you the most? In what way?
11. Which minister influenced you the most? In what way?
12. What questions did you have as a child/teen about your faith? Who gave you any answers?

13. Was there any camp or special meeting that affected you spiritually?
14. Did you read the Bible as a teen?
15. Did you memorize any Scripture as a child or teen? Do you remember any of that Scripture now?
16. As a child, if you could have asked God any questions, what would they have been?
17. As a teen, if you could have asked God any questions, what would they have been?
18. If you could ask God any questions now, what would they be?
19. What would have helped you more spiritually when you were growing up?
20. Did anyone disappoint you spiritually as a child? If so, how has that impacted you as an adult?
21. When you went through difficult times as a child or teen, how did that affect your faith?
22. What has been the greatest spiritual experience of your life?

Probably the most important question is, How important is prayer together for you as a couple? On a scale of 0 to 10, it's got to be a 10. No other way to put it! Rather than thinking of prayer together as a couple as a duty, a drudgery or a negative mandate, think of it as the gift from God that it is.

Over the years, I've collected statements or quotes from others whose words have encouraged and challenged me in my own marriage. Think about the following statements about prayer:

Prayer is an awareness of the presence of a holy and loving God in one's life, and an awareness of God's relations to one's husband or wife. Prayer is listening to God, a valuable lesson in learning to listen to one another.

It is only when a husband and wife pray together before God that they find the secret of true harmony; that the difference in their temperaments, their ideas and their tastes enriches their home instead of endangering it.

Lines open to God are invariably open to one another, for a person cannot be genuinely open to God and closed to his mate. Praying together especially reduces the sense of competiveness in marriage, at the same time enhancing the sense of completeness.

Scripture also tells us to pray:

As for me, far be it from me that I should sin against the Lord by ending my prayers for you; and I will continue to teach you those things which are good and right (1 Sam. 12:23, *TLB*).

You haven't tried this before, [but begin now]. Ask, using my name, and you will receive, and your cup of joy will overflow (John 16:24, *TLB*).

Don't worry about anything; instead, pray about everything; tell God your needs and don't forget to thank him for his answers (Phil. 4:6, *TLB*).

Always keep on praying (1 Thess. 5:17, *TLB*).

Admit your faults to one another and pray for each other so that you may be healed. The earnest prayer of a righteous man has great power and wonderful results (Jas. 5:16, *TLB*).

GUIDELINES FOR PRAYING TOGETHER

How do you start praying together as a couple? Why not begin by praying by yourself for your partner? Ask God to bless and to lead your spouse. I know couples that call one another during the day to tell them they're praying for each other. Other couples ask each other before they part for the day, "How can I pray for you today?" At the conclusion of the day, it gives you something to discuss. When I was on a trip, I found notes in my clothes from Joyce, stating that she was praying for me.

The easiest way to begin praying together is to take the time and set a time to do it. I've heard so many say that with their schedules it's almost impossible. I disagree. Creativity and flexibility can make it happen. You can put your arms around each other for 30 seconds and pray before you leave for the day, or after dinner. Couples can pray together over the phone when they're apart. Creative couples write their prayers and send them to each other via email. With cellular phones couples can pray while driving (hopefully with their eyes open) and make contact in this way. You can text your prayers to one another.

When you start praying together at home, perhaps it's best just to share some requests and then pray silently together. There is no threat in this.

Praying aloud is something you grow into. It may take awhile to develop a comfort level. Communication doesn't always have to be vocal. We're bombarded with noise all the time. Sometimes couples struggle with audible prayer, because they don't communicate very much with each other or anyone else. Or one spouse feels that the other is much more articulate and fluent. It could be true, but this is not a time for comparison or competitive endeavor. It's time for learning to accept who you are. I always felt that my wife's prayers were much more detailed and in-depth than mine. But that never hindered me from praying aloud.

I like the journey that Charles and Martha Shedd experienced in learning to pray together.

> We would take turns telling each other things we'd like to pray about. Then holding hands, we would pray each in our own way, silently.
>
> This was the beginning of praying together that lasted. Naturally, through the years we've learned to pray in everyday language. Seldom with "thee." We laugh, we argue, we enjoy. We hurt together, cry together, wonder together. Together we tune our friendship to the Friend of friends.
>
> Do we still pray silently together? Often. Some groanings of the spirit go better in the silence.
>
> "I've been feeling anxious lately and I don't know why. Will you listen while I tell you what I can? Then let's pray about the known and unknown in silence."
>
> "This is one of my super days. So good. Yet somehow I can't find words to tell you. Let's thank the Lord together in quiet."
>
> Negatives, positives, woes, celebrations, shadowy things—all these, all kinds of things we share in prayer. Aloud we share what we can. Without the vocals we share those things not ready yet for words.

Why would this approach have the feel of the real? Almost from the first we knew we'd discovered an authentic new dimension.

In becoming best friends with each other, we are becoming best friends with the Lord.

And the more we sought his friendship, the more we were becoming best friends with each other.[5]

One of the other reasons for praying silently has to do with the unique way God has created us in both our gender and personality differences. Most of us men prefer to put things on the back burner and think about them for a while. If we have the opportunity to reflect on what we want to pray about, we're eventually more open to praying. Extroverts find it easier to pray aloud because they think aloud; whereas, introverts need to think things through silently in their minds before sharing. Silent prayer is less threatening. Some prefer reflecting for a while first and writing out their prayer. There's nothing wrong with this.

THE RESULTS OF PRAYING TOGETHER

There are benefits to praying together. When a man and woman marry, they no longer think and act as a single person. It's no longer "I" but "we." All life is lived in connection with another person. Everything you do affects this significant person. You're a team of two, and when both of you participate, you function better. When you confront problems and crises in your life (and you will), it's a source of comfort and support to know that here's another person who will pray for you and with you. When you're struggling financially, or with problems at work;

when you have tough decisions to make, or a medical crisis; to be able to share the burden with your spouse lightens the load.

Couples need to pray together for the health of their marriage. When you married, you entered into a high-risk adventure. The vows you took at your wedding will be attacked on all sides. Praying together will make your marriage stronger as well as help to protect you from reacting sinfully toward your spouse.

Scripture's promise about the effectiveness of prayer includes the prayers of married couples. Jesus said, "Again, I tell you that if two of you on earth agree about anything you ask for, it will be done for you by my Father in heaven. For where two or three come together in my name, there am I with them" (Matt. 18:19-20).

Couples who have prayer lists and see the results of answered prayers will be encouraged as they see how God works in their lives.

When couples pray together, it has an impact on disagreements, conflicts and anger expressed toward each other. When you see your spouse as a child of God, valuable and precious in His sight, someone He sent His Son to die for, wouldn't that have an effect on how you pray for him or her? In the book *If Two Shall Agree* by Carey Moore and Pamela Roswell Moore, Carey put it plainly:

> To place Christ at the center of our homes means, of course, to tell Him, "You are our God," not just at prayer time but all day long. I cannot be careless or insensitive in what I say to Pam and then pray with her. Nor can either of us treat anyone else rudely or engage in gossip and criticism or allow conceit and pride to rule in our

relations with others, and expect God to hear our prayers at the end of the day.[6]

Have you ever felt like this when it comes to prayer? "I just don't know what to say when I pray. Sometimes I'm at a loss for words."

If you've ever felt this way, you're not alone. We've all felt like this at some point. Often it's when we attempt to pray that we become very conscious of a spiritual struggle in our life. As we sit down to pray, our minds wander. Every few minutes we sneak a look at the clock to see if we've prayed enough. Has that happened to you when you pray alone? It has to me. But it's interesting that when couples pray together, it happens less often.

The Holy Spirit is God's answer when we don't know how to pray. You and I cannot pray as we ought to pray. We are often crippled in our prayer lives. That's where the work of the Holy Spirit really comes into play. He helps us in our prayer lives by showing us what we should pray for and how we ought to pray. That's quite a promise!

J.B. Phillips translates Romans 8:26-27 in this manner:

The Spirit also helps us in our present limitations. For example, we do not know how to pray worthy as sons of God, but his Spirit within us is actually praying for us in those agonizing longings which never find words. And God who knows the heart's secrets understands, of course, the Spirit's intention as he prays for those who love God.

One of your callings in marriage is to assist your partner when he or she needs help. You are always to be listening for a call for assistance. Similarly, there is someone looking out for us when we need help in our prayer lives: the Holy Spirit. There are several specific ways that He helps us.

First, *the Spirit intercedes for you* when you are oppressed by problems in life or when you feel down on yourself. He brings you to the place where you can pray. Your ability to begin praying is prompted and produced by the working of the Holy Spirit within you. There may be times when all you can do is sigh or sob inwardly. Even this kind of prayer is the result of the Spirit's work.

Second, *the Spirit reveals to your mind what you should pray for.* He makes you conscious of such things as your needs, your lack of faith, your fears, your need to be obedient, and so on. He helps you identify your spiritual needs and bring them into the presence of God. He helps you by diminishing your fears, increasing your faith and strengthening your hope. If you're at a loss to know what you need to pray for about your partner or even what to pray for together, ask the Holy Spirit to intercede for you.

Third, *the Spirit guides you by directing your thoughts* to the promises of God's Word that are best suited to your needs. He helps you realize the truth of God's promises. The discernment you lack is supplied to you by the Spirit. Perhaps you're looking for a verse to apply to your marriage. Again, help is available through the Spirit.

Finally, *the Spirit helps you pray in the right way.* He helps you sift through your prayers and bring them into conformity with the purpose of prayer.

When you experience a crisis, it may be difficult for you to talk. But you and your spouse can hold each other and quietly allow the Holy Spirit to pray for you. This is called the silent prayer of the heart.

When you are having difficulty praying, remember that you have someone to draw on for strength in developing your prayer life.

When is the best time for a couple to pray? You decide for yourself. It may vary or it may be set. There will be all kinds of interferences from the phone and TV, and child interruptions and exhaustion. But a commitment to be faithful in prayer can override excuses. James Dobson shares a situation he and his wife, Shirley, experienced:

> I'll never forget the time a few years ago when our daughter had just learned to drive. . . . It was during this era that Shirley and I covenanted between us to pray for our son and daughter at the close of every day. Not only were we concerned about the risk of an automobile accident, but we were also aware of so many other dangers that lurk out there in a city like Los Angeles. . . . That's one reason we found ourselves on our knees each evening, asking for divine protection for the teenagers whom we love so much.
>
> One night we were particularly tired and collapsed into bed without our benedictory prayer. We were almost asleep before Shirley's voice pierced the night. "Jim," she said, "we haven't prayed for our kids yet today."
>
> I admit it was very difficult for me to pull my 6' 2" frame out of the warm bed that night. Nevertheless, we got on our knees and offered a prayer for our children's safety, placing them in the hands of the Father once more.
>
> Later we learned that (our daughter) Danae and a girlfriend had gone to a fast-food establishment and

bought hamburgers and Cokes. They drove up the road a few miles and were sitting in the car eating the meal when a policeman drove by, shining his spotlight in all directions, obviously looking for someone.

In a few minutes, Danae and her friend heard a "clunk" from under the car. They looked at one another nervously and felt another sharp bump. Then a man crawled out from under the car. He was unshaven and looked like he had been on the street for weeks. He tugged at the door attempting to open it. Thank God, it was locked. Danae quickly started the car and drove off . . . no doubt at record speed.

Later when we checked the timing of this incident, we realized that Shirley and I had been on our knees at the precise moment of danger. Our prayers were answered. Our daughter and her friend were safe![7]

We keep appointments with others and make sure we're always available for certain TV shows. Similarly, when you establish a specific time or pattern for prayer, and keep to it consistently, it becomes a regular part of your life. Some couples pray in their kitchen, family room, bedroom, car or on walks. Work out what's best for you.

Sometimes it helps to read prayers out loud that others have written. For years (ever since college!) off and on I've used a book of daily prayers by John Baillie called *A Diary of Private Prayer*. Reading the psalms aloud can be a prayer. You can pray about everything, and I mean everything.

Recently, I found a fascinating resource that personalizes passages of Scripture into prayers for a husband and wife. It is called *Praying God's Will for My Marriage* by Lee Roberts. It simply takes passages of Scripture and rewords them. By reading these aloud for a while, any couple could learn to do this for themselves. Here is a sampling:

> I pray that my spouse and I will be swift to hear, slow to speak, slow to wrath, for the wrath of man does not produce the righteousness of God (James 1:19-20).

> I pray that my spouse and I will always love the Lord our God with all our heart, with all our soul, with all our mind, and with all our strength and that we love our neighbor as ourselves (Mark 12:30-31).

> I pray that when my spouse and I face an obstacle we always remember that God has said, "Not by might nor by power, but by my Spirit" (Zechariah 4:6).

> I pray that if my spouse and I lack wisdom, we ask it of You, God, who gives to all liberally and without reproach and that it will be given to us (James 1:5).

> I pray that because freely my spouse and I have received, freely we will give (Matthew 10:8).

> I pray, O God, that You have comforted my spouse and me and will have mercy on our afflictions (Isaiah 49:13).

> I pray that my spouse and I will bless You, the Lord, at all times; and that your praise continually be in our mouths (Psalm 34:1).

I pray to You, God, that my spouse and I will present
our bodies a living sacrifice, holy and acceptable to
God, which is our reasonable service. I pray also that
we will not be conformed to this work, but transformed
by the renewing of our minds, that we may prove what
is good and acceptable and the perfect will of God (Romans 12:1-2).[8]

Prayer is one of the best ways to experience closeness. When
your wife is discouraged, go up to her and hug her, and pray a
one-line prayer of support. You can do this with your eyes open
and looking her in the face. When she is upset or stressed, you
could touch her on the arm and pray, "Lord, give strength and
peace; lift the pressure and show me how to support my loved
one." This in itself can be supportive.

What has prayer done for couples? Listen to what some
have said:

"We both feel that communication with God deep-
ens . . . the spiritual and emotional intimacy we share
with one another," one couple wrote, "Prayer is the
means by which we build upon the Lord's love for us as
the foundation of our marriage, and the medium by
which we achieve spiritual agreement (Amos 3:3). The
goal of our prayer life is spiritual unity, emotional one-
ness and marital harmony."

"Sharing our spiritual lives," said Joel and Maria Shuler,
"is one of the ways we work at being truly intimate. We
believe that God wants us to be one, to be united in every
way possible. Our total couple intimacy is enhanced by

our couple prayer. With God, we are at our most vulnerable. It is a gift we give to each other, a special time." This is from a couple who found praying together "awkward" at first.

Joel and Maria are Catholics and have been committed to prayer together since Joel's conversion from Judaism some 10 years ago. "At first," they recall, "we had to pray mostly traditional prayers" from a book, but Maria knew them so well she would run ahead of Joel. At one point their inability to pray at the same pace struck them as very funny. "We laughed so hard we couldn't continue with the prayer, but the experience freed us up to be more comfortable and natural before the Lord," Maria says.

"We believe that God wants us to be united in mind, heart and body. We work toward unity in every area of our lives, and have much to glean when we share our faith and spirituality with each other. We see how we complement and learn from each other, and thank God for bringing us together. God, Joel and I are like a three-ply cord that is woven and intertwined."[9]

If you want to bring out the best in your wife, be the spiritual leader.

If you want to bring out the best in your wife, pray for her.

If you want to bring out the best in your wife, pray together.

DISCOVER THE ENCOURAGER IN YOU

1. Do you pray on a regular basis for your wife, and with your wife? Do you read God's Word together as well? If you do not, why not?

2. How have you defined "intimacy" to this point in your life? Has your definition changed based on what you have read?

3. Why is spiritual intimacy in marriage so important to the health of your total relationship?

4. Can you imagine the effect on your marriage relationship when you use God's Word as your prayers? Why not try it for a one-month experiment, and then note the difference it has made in your marriage.

5. Prayer is such an encouraging way to experience God's work in your life. So what better way to apply all that you have learned about how to bring out the best in your wife than to ask God to guide your steps as you cultivate your home environment? Today, ask God to help you find new ways to encourage your wife.

Prayer of Commitment

Father, I want to encourage my wife, but in so many ways I don't know how. However, I do know that Your Holy Spirit can instruct me and guide me in my efforts to build up my relationship with my wife and to be the leader that You've called me to be. Help me to get past any ingrained habits of reacting and any wrong attitudes. I specifically ask You to help me with [list any specific issues]. Amen.

9

Some
Concluding Thoughts

THIS IS NOT AN EASY BOOK TO WRITE FOR ONE SIMPLE REASON: I am no longer married. I was for 48 years. I wanted it to continue, for it was a good and fulfilling marriage. Joyce was a loving, gracious woman who deeply cared for her Lord and others. Instead of living longer and perhaps experiencing 50 or even 60 years, God had other plans. On September 15, 2007, He called Joyce home. So after all these years of living "with," I've had to learn to live "without." During my months of intense grief, I journaled. My thoughts and feelings became a book, *Reflections of a Grieving Spouse.*

There was one section that I believe fits into the conclusion of this book. This is part of my own personal journey. I hope it generates some thinking on your part about what you can do with the years you have left with your wife.

NEVER ENOUGH

In life, the phrase "never enough" resides in most of us. Some would admit to it, whereas others would deny its presence. Who wouldn't want more of whatever brings satisfaction or delight to our lives. For some it's a constant nagging sense of dissatisfaction, which diminishes the benefit of what they have received, while for others it's because what they experienced was so wonderful they want it to continue if possible.

Parents are heard to tell their children, "You are never satisfied."

Spouses are heard to tell their spouses, "You are never satisfied."

The "never enough" desire can create greed or generosity, selfishness or compassion.

We're admonished to have this feeling by what others have said to us. "You could have studied (practiced, worked out, listened, paid attention) more" and we incorporate their admonition into our own belief system.

Sometimes we wonder if we couldn't have done more, if we really had done enough. I wonder . . .

Saving Private Ryan sent me down this pathway in my mind, and it's come back from time to time over the past few months of my grief over Joyce. In the movie by the same name, a squad of soldiers is deployed to find this man in order to bring him home since his other brothers have already been killed. They eventually find him, but in the battles several of the soldiers are killed, including the captain portrayed by Tom Hanks. As the captain lies dying on a bridge, and the battle has been won, he whispers to Private Ryan, "Earn this . . . earn this," and so Ryan goes through his life with those words ringing forever in the back of his mind: "Men died for you. Live up to their sacrifice for you. Don't let your life be wasted, for it was bought by the blood of others."

How similar to our own spiritual redemption—purchased by the blood of another. At the conclusion of this film, Private Ryan is elderly and takes his family to Europe to visit the gravesite of his captain. His face reflects his memories as well as his feelings, and his unspoken question of wonderment is, "Did I earn this? Did I do enough? Could I have done more?"

As his wife walks up to join him, with a sad, painful expression on his face, he turns to her and says, "Tell me I've led a good life. Tell me I'm a good man." Perhaps these were thoughts that haunted him over the past decades. He could have asked himself these questions thousands of times, like many of us do. But now he voiced them, for he wanted to hear the affirmation, "You are," which he did.

Don't we all have questions of wonderment about ourselves—who we are, who we could be, what we could have done, or what we will be able to do?

When a loved one dies, there will be questions. Was I a good husband to this woman? What could I have done differently? More of or less of? Sometimes these questions reflect just that—a question. In some cases, they're evidence of regret or a wish that something could have been more or less or could have occurred or didn't occur.

I've heard some say, "I have no regrets." Well, perhaps; but deep within us, no matter how much we gave or did, or who we were, is really that sense of satisfaction. A conviction that *it was* enough. Or could we, along with the belief "I really did all that I could or wanted to give," also have that feeling "Did I really do enough? Could I have done more?"

I do. I wonder about many things. It may have been enough for us, but was it enough for the others? For that's what really counts. Was it enough for Joyce? Was it sufficient? Could I have done more or less in some areas? I wish I knew. I don't and won't know.

Like Private Ryan, we live with wonder and unanswered questions.

And it's not just questions that arise about the last months of being together, but over the 48 years of togetherness.

And so I struggle with the same questions: Did I do enough? Could I have done more? Some say these are futile questions, for how can anyone formulate an answer that is factual rather than emotional? But perhaps that's why the question needs to be voiced, to be asked—to give words to the emotion.

The benefit is probably not in any answer but in the introspective process leading to the question. And so I ask, What more could I have done, as Private Ryan asked . . .

- Was I attentive enough?
- Did I listen to you enough?
- How could I have helped and supported you more in your times of confusion?
- Did I walk with you enough during the "terrible" days?
- Did I pray with you enough? No, definitely not.
- Did I turn the radio up enough in the darkness of night so you could hear the music you loved? Oh, how you loved the Word expressed in music!
- Did I encourage you enough in your uniqueness as a person?
- Did I encourage you enough in your art?
- How could I have helped you more with Matthew?[1]

Endnotes

Chapter 1: Believe in Your Wife

1. Lysa Jenkinson, *Capture Her Heart* (Chicago, IL: Moody Press, 2002), p. 93.
2. Alan Loy McGinnis, *The Friendship Factor* (Minneapolis, MN: Augsburg Publishing House, 1979), pp. 101-102.
3. Lee Blaine, *The Power Principle* (New York: Simon & Schuster, 1997), pp. 161-162.
4. John C. Maxwell, *Be a People Person* (Wheaton, IL: Victor Books, 1994), p. 137.
5. Ibid., pp. 134-135.
6. Blaine, *The Power Principle,* pp. 125-126.
7. Don Dinkmeyer and Lewis Lasney, *The Encouragement Book* (Englewood Cliffs, NJ: Prentice Hall, 1980), pp. 50-83, adapted.
8. Dr. Richard Matteson and Janis Long Harris, *What if I Married the Wrong Person?* (Minneapolis, MN: 1996), pp. 116-117.

Chapter 3: Wives Speak Out

1. One Hundred Women with Dan True, *What Do Women Want from Men?* (Grass Valley, CA: Blue Dolphin Publishing, 1994), pp. 42-43.
2. Ibid., p. 129.
3. Clifford I. Notorius and Howard J. Markman, *We Can Work It Out: How to Solve Conflicts, Save Your Marriage, and Strengthen Your Love for Each Other* (New York: GP Putnam's Sons, 1993), pp. 20-21.
4. Ibid., pp. 123-124, adapted.
5. Gregory Papcak, MSW, *The Exceptional Seven Percent* (New York: Citadel Press, 2000), pp. 164-167.
6. True, *What Do Women Want from Men?* pp. 209-211.

Chapter 4: Understand Your Wife

1. Barbara Rosberg, *Connecting with Your Wife* (Wheaton, IL: Tyndale House, 2003), pp. xvii-xviii.
2. Phillip C. McGraw, Ph.D., *Relationship Rescue* (New York: Hyperion, 2000), p. 221.
3. Scott Halzman, M.D., with Theresa Fox, *The Secrets of Happily Married Men* (New York: Jossey-Bass, 2006), adapted, pp. 81-86.
4. Ibid., pp. 87-88.
5. Rosberg, *Connecting with Your Wife,* p. 58.
6. Lillian Glass, Ph.D., *Complete Idiot's Guide to Understanding Men and Women* (Indianapolis, IN: Alpha Books, 2000), adapted, p. 33.
7. Halzman, *The Secrets of Happily Married Men,* adapted, pp. 172-176.
8. John Gray, Ph.D., *Mars and Venus Together Forever* (New York: Harper & Row, 1996), pp. 148-149.
9. Willard F. Harley, Jr., *His Needs, Her Needs* (Grand Rapids, MI: Zondervan, 1986), pp. 77-78.
10. David L. Leucke, *The Relationship Manual* (Columbia, MD: The Relationship Institute, 1981), adapted, p. 25.

Chapter 5: Romancing Your Wife

1. *Webster's New Collegiate Dictionary*, p. 996
2. Lucy Sanna and Kathy Miller, *How to Romance the Woman You Love—The Way She Wants You To!* (Rocklin, CA: Prima Publishing, 1995), p. xvii.
3. Ibid., pp. 184-185.
4. Ibid., adapted, p. 158.
5. Ibid., pp. 158-159.
6. Joseph Dillow, *Solomon on Sex* (Nashville, TN: Thomas Nelson, 1977).
7. Willard F. Harley, Jr., *His Needs, Her Needs* (Grand Rapids, MI: Zondervan, 1986), p. 38.
8. Ibid., p. 47.
9. Leo F. Buscaglia, *Loving Each Other* (New York: Random House, Inc. Faucett Columbine, 1984), adapted, pp. 135-146.
10. Original source unknown.
11. David Luecke, *The Relationship Manual* (Columbia, MD: The Relationship Institute, 1981), adapted, p 74.

Chapter 6: God's Plan for Husbands

1. Gary Thomas, *Sacred Marriage* (Grand Rapids, MI: Zondervan, 2000), p. 33
2. Ed Young, *The Ten Commandments of Marriage* (Chicago: Moody Press, 2003), p. 11.
3. Stormie Omartian, *The Power of a Praying Husband* (Eugene, OR: Harvest House Publishers, 2007), p. 23.
4. Bryan Chapell, *Each for the Other* (Grand Rapids, MI: Baker Books, 1988), adapted, pp. 47-50.
5. Ibid,, p. 51.
6. Ibid., p. 52.
7. Omartian, *The Power of a Praying Husband*, p. 33.
8. Ibid., pp. 35-41.
9. H. Norman Wright, *One Marriage Under God* (Portland, OR: Multnomah Publishers, 2005), adapted, pp. 19-36.

Chapter 7: Questions Men Ask

1. Georgie Witkin-Lanoil, *The Male Stress Syndrome* (New York: New Market Press, 1986), p. 129.
2. James G. T. Fairfield, *When You Don't Agree* (Scottsdale, PA: Herald Press, 1977).
3. Jeanette Lauer and Robert Lauer, *Til Death Do We Part* (New York: Routledge, 1986), adapted, p. 158.
4. Ed and Carol Neuenschwander, *Two Friends in Love* (Portland, OR: Multnomah Press, 1986), p. 108.
5. Norm Wright, *Communication: Key to Your Marriage* (Ventura, CA: Regal, 2000), pp. 118-119.
6. Michael McGill, *The McGill Report on Male Intimacy* (San Francisco: Harper & Row, 1985), p. 74.
7. Bill and Pam Ferrel, *Men Are Like Waffles—Women Are Like Spaghetti* (Eugene, OR: Harvest House, 2001), pp. 28-30.

Chapter 8: The Power of a Praying Man

1. Donald R. Harvey, *The Spiritually Intimate Marriage* (Grand Rapids, MI: Fleming H. Revell, 1991), p. 24.

2. Ibid., p. 24.
3. Howard and Jeanne Hendricks, general editors, with LaVonne Neff, *Husbands and Wives* (Wheaton, IL: Victor Books, 1988), p. 158.
4. Harvey, *The Spiritually Intimate Marriage,* adapted, pp. 54-56.
5. From "How to Start and Keep It Going," by Charlie and Martha Shedd, cited by Fritz Ridenour in "Praying Together," *The Marriage Collection* (Grand Rapids, MI: Zondervan Publishers, 1989), pp. 442-443.
6. Carey Moore and Pamela Roswell Moore, *If Two Shall Agree* (Grand Rapids, MI: Chosen Books, Baker Book House, 1992).
7. James C. Dobson, *Love for a Lifetime* (Portland, OR: Multnomah Press, 1987), pp. 51-52.
8. Lee Roberts, *Praying God's Will for My Marriage* (Nashville: Thomas Nelson, 1994), pp. 1,9,19,28,115,162,227,267.
9. Moore and Roswell Moore, *If Two Shall Agree,* pp. 194-195.

Chapter 9: Some Concluding Thoughts
1. H. Norman Wright, *Reflections of a Grieving Spouse* (Eugene, OR: Harvest House, 2009).

Are You Bringing Out the Best in Your Husband?

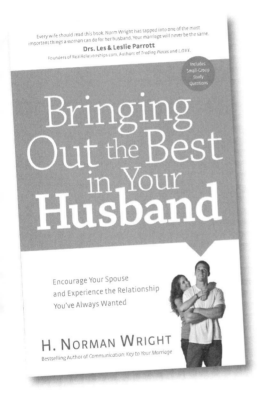

Bringing Out the Best in Your Husband
H. Norman Wright
ISBN 978.08307.52188
ISBN 08307.52188

Bookstore shelves are crammed with claims about how you can get what you want out of your man . . . but affectionate, long-lasting relationships thrive when the tables are turned: when each spouse focuses on giving, not getting! In *Bringing Out the Best in Your Husband*, you'll find biblical and practical, proven ways to make your marriage a safe haven of encouragement, respect and love. Bestselling author and family therapist H. Norman Wright includes countless true-life stories from men who share their fears and from women who long to understand their spouse's needs and desires, and who are learning how to unlock their husband's heart with acceptance, support and affirmation. Based on his experience counseling thousands of couples over more than 40 years, Dr. Wright understands the tremendous impact a wife has on her husband—and he shows you how to turn that impact into a loving, joy-filled marriage that stands the test of time!

Also Available from
H. Norman Wright

Communication: Key to Your Marriage
Practical Guide to Creating a Happy, Fulfilling Relationship
ISBN 978.08307.25335
ISBN 08307.25334

Starting Out Together
A Devotional for Dating or Engaged Couples
ISBN 978.08307.19013
ISBN 08307.19016

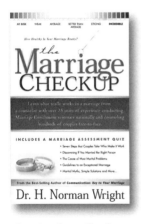

The Marriage Checkup
How Healthy Is Your Marriage Really?
ISBN 978.08307.30698
ISBN 08307.30699

Now That You're Engaged
The Keys to Building a Strong, Lasting Relationship
ISBN 978.08307.39219
ISBN 08307.39211